'This is a [...]
brotherhoo[...]
a story of a c[...]

— GG ALCOCK, bestselling author of *KasiNomic Revolution*,
KasiNomics and *Third World Child*

'From tracking leopards for Big Five-hungry tourists to being confronted with the realities of our racially prejudiced society, Van den Heever candidly writes about the accomplishments and adversities he and Mhlongo have experienced over their 20-odd years as tracking partners. A collection of cool *bos* stories as much as it is an eloquent meditation on a fragmented country, *Changing a Leopard's Spots* will appeal to aspiring Louis Liebenbergs and perceptive South Africans alike.'

— MILA DE VILLIERS, *Sunday Times* Lifestyle Magazine

'If you love the bush, adore wild animal stories or are simply curious about the life of a guide, this book is for you.'

— TIANA CLINE, *Popular Mechanics*

'Through the accounts of Van den Heever's and Mhlongo's adventures and their deep soul-searching discussions, this book also becomes a motivational guide on how trust and reliance can exist not only for survival but out of a curiosity for "the other".'

— ORIELLE BERRY, *Cape Argus*

'An inspiring story of an unbreakable bond between two wildlife trackers.'

— ERNS GRUNDLING, *GO!* magazine

Hi Fabiana,

Changing a Leopard's Spots

Eta V

Thank you for
listening to our story!

June 2023

For the three most exceptional women I know:
Pippa, Bella and Sophie

Changing a Leopard's Spots

The Adventures of Two Wildlife Trackers

Alex van den Heever
with Renias Mhlongo

MACMILLAN

First published in 2020
by Pan Macmillan South Africa

This edition published in 2023
by Pan Macmillan South Africa
Private Bag X19
Northlands
Johannesburg
2116
www.panmacmillan.co.za

ISBN 978-1-77010-843-1
e-ISBN 978-1-77010-844-8

© 2020, 2023 Alex van den Heever and Renias Mhlongo

All rights reserved. No part of this publication may be reproduced, stored in or introduced into a retrieval system, or transmitted, in any form or by any means (electronic, mechanical, photocopying, recording or otherwise), without the prior written permission of the publisher. Any person who does any unauthorised act in relation to this publication may be liable to criminal prosecution and civil claims for damages.

Editing by Jane Bowman
Proofreading by Sean Fraser
Design and typesetting by Triple M Design, Johannesburg
Cover design by publicide
Front cover leopard photograph by James Tyrrell
Printed by novus print, a division of Novus Holdings

Contents

A defining moment 1
Failing is the winning 19
Under an ebony tree 40
Welcome to Dixie 55
Realising Renias 71
Lessons from Eric 89
Wearing the tag 107
Life with Renias 118
The gift of Aloe 132
A poacher at heart 151
The elusive nature of trust 169
The path of a tracker 191
The realisation of a dream 207
Calming elusive predators 226
Tracking racial prejudice 245

Appendix: The five elements of tracking 261
Further reading 271
Acknowledgements 273
Tracking success by Alex & Renias 277

A defining moment

I was at the wheel of the Land Rover with six Canadian guests in the back, cruising towards leopard country. Renias Mhlongo, my colleague and the tracker I was assigned to work with, was perched on the tracker's seat located above the front left wheel, scanning the ground intently. It was a hot summer's morning and I had not slept well due to the extreme humidity. As the brand-new guide, as part of my 'initiation', I was not permitted to use an air conditioner in my room and listening to the gentle hum of the senior guy's aircon next door made it worse. I would lie in bed, sweating, trying to pretend I had one too. But my lack of sleep was not the only issue; that morning was the final game drive for this family of guests who had saved for many years for their one-and-only trip to Africa, and it was up to Renias and me to find a leopard.

The family had chosen Londolozi because of its world-famous leopard viewing. Every magazine article and brochure they had seen about this private game reserve was full of images of leopards:

leopards in trees, leopards with cubs, fighting leopards, hunting leopards; you name it, the best leopard viewing in the world is at Londolozi.

These people wanted to see a leopard. Their friends had visited two years before and had seen four different leopards, including one on a kill. So it was understandable that they were beginning to show signs of frustration and irritation when by day three it didn't look like we had any chance of finding one. What made it even more stressful was that the eldest son of the family owned a start-up travel agency in Colorado and my general manager had given me the express instruction to ensure that they 'see everything'.

The night before, as I walked back to my room from the boma after supper, the head ranger told me that the son had asked whether it was possible for them to go out with another guide and tracker the next morning. 'Are you sure Alex and Renias are up to it?' he'd apparently enquired. This unnerved me and brought on a feeling of pressure that I had not experienced before. The life of a guide wasn't supposed to be like this. I had never anticipated that my dream job of living and working in the bushveld would become so stressful. I started to feel I was too young, too inexperienced and simply not up to the task.

I bypassed my room and headed straight to Renias's house, woke him up and explained the situation to him. 'Tell the guests we are leaving at 4am tomorrow,' he offhandedly muttered.

'But what's the plan?' I asked. He said he would sleep on it and give me an answer in the morning.

A DEFINING MOMENT

'Maybe a plan will come in my dreams tonight,' he said, smiling at me. I was not convinced.

For some reason, I felt a lot better the next morning and I was determined not only to find a leopard, but to give these guests the best game drive experience that I could possibly deliver. That sentiment was not to last long. 'Ahiyi Tugwaan,' said Renias 30 seconds before the guests arrived in the car park for their final drive. I had been waiting for him for fifteen minutes and had desperately wanted to discuss some kind of plan with him before we departed on our game drive. We didn't get that opportunity.

The Tugwaan is a dry riverbed that runs east to west through the southern extent of the Londolozi area and that is where Renias wanted to go. Although it forms the core territory of several individual leopards, many of them were not accustomed to people and vehicles. You often saw the evidence of old impala kills hanging in the trees, killed by leopards, but you had to work hard to actually see a leopard in that area. It is rocky with long grass and dotted with isolated groves of acacia trees. A few weeks earlier I had dislocated my thumb when the wheel of the old Land Rover collided with an unseen rock in the grass causing the steering wheel to spin out of control, smashing my finger in the process. So I wasn't a fan of the southern area around the Tugwaan.

There was, however, a single young male called the Tugwaan Young Male who was reasonably relaxed. Renias had relayed, in Shangaan, which I couldn't speak or understand much of, that on his way to meet us, he had walked past the workshop and Michael, a tractor driver, had mentioned that he had seen a young leopard near the Tugwaan donga the day before. The problem was that the Tugwaan donga is 10 kilometres in length and to look for just one young leopard in an area of 15 000 hectares along several kilometres of riverbed sounded like a terrible plan to me!

The guests were now in the vehicle so I had no option but to go along with Renias's idea. Now we're in the hands of a tractor driver, I thought, as we pulled out of the camp in the half-light. Renias was winging it. All the other guides had told me what a great tracker he was, a 'Londolozi legend', one said. But at that moment I had no reason to trust that was true. I felt he was being far too contemptuous about the situation and it made me feel vulnerable.

Our guests' expectations weighed on me. As far as I was concerned, we had important people with us who had paid a lot of money to come to Londolozi and I was fearful of failing them. I considered for a while that the little reputation I had was about to be smashed. I also realised how much I relied on Renias and that should I wish to avoid a situation like this in the future, I needed to improve my own bush skills. Maybe I should train to become a professional tracker, I thought to myself. I assumed, with the arrogance of ignorance, it would be a fairly easy process.

As the wheels of the Land Rover dipped into the sand of the Tugwaan dry riverbed, Renias started to bang on the bonnet and then said to me, 'Hima.' Stop. He gestured nonchalantly to the ground and hopped off. I got out and walked around the front of the vehicle to have a look. All I could see was a faint and completely nondescript smudge in the soil. He circled it with his finger and told me it was a track left by the Tugwaan female, the mother of

A DEFINING MOMENT

the Tugwaan Young Male. My week-long tracking course three months before had obviously not prepared me to see leopard tracks and I couldn't make out much, let alone a track. I sat hunched over the mark for a good few minutes before Renias, anxious to get tracking, took a small twig and outlined the track for me. Helping make it look like a perfect leopard spoor was Renias's first 'lesson' for me. By destroying the original impression, I could see what he had drawn. I felt frustrated as I needed to see the track without it being highlighted. My impatience was clouding my receptivity and I wasn't even aware of it.

Again, doubt started to flood into my thoughts. Was this genuinely a fresh track of the Tugwaan female leopard? How could Renias possibly make such a detailed interpretation from such an indistinct piece of evidence? The Canadians were at this point standing up in the vehicle staring down at us, no doubt witnessing my uncertainty. When one of them asked what we were looking at, and I answered 'a fresh leopard track', I sensed my words came out with little conviction. They must have thought I was clueless.

I looked up and Renias was signalling to me from a distance to bring the rifle from the vehicle. He had already started following the trail of the Tugwaan female in the time that I had been concerned about how I was being perceived. Little did I know at this very early stage of my career, and in terms of life lessons, who Renias really was and the enormous footsteps I was about to follow in.

Londolozi Game Reserve, through its documentary-making owner John Varty and a small group of skilled wildlife trackers, began tracking leopards there in the late 1970s in order to habituate them. John wanted to capture their behaviour on film and the guides desperately wanted to be able show these highly elusive cats to the guests staying at the Londolozi camp. Through extreme patience and with tenacious and skilful tracking, this band of bushveld mavericks achieved what no one had ever done before – settle wild leopards so that people from around the world could view them in their natural environment. Renias was a member of that team.

In the 1980s, Londolozi shot to international acclaim and the leopards were rewarded with a secure piece of pristine wildlife real estate on which to live. Prior to a successful ecotourism venture, the greater Londolozi area was a bankrupt cattle ranch with little economic viability. The leopards, and indeed all the other classic African animals, were the reason why vast swathes of land were restored under wildlife in the then Eastern Transvaal Lowveld. The work with leopards of this non-conforming and eccentric team of trackers at Londolozi created a ripple effect throughout the Sabi Sands Game Reserve, on which Londolozi is situated, which ultimately caused it to become one of the most coveted safari destinations in southern Africa. Today, other world-famous private lodges such as Singita and Sabi Sabi are all members of the Sabi Sands Game Reserve.

When the trackers conducted their habituation in the late 1980s, the Tugwaan female leopard was the most cantankerous leopard at Londolozi. Some of the senior guides had told me frightening stories of her charging completely unprovoked, sometimes causing guests to hyperventilate in absolute fear. A tracker told me how she almost clawed him off the front of the Land Rover he was on. Interestingly, she was the daughter of the original Mother Leopard who had produced nine litters of cubs over a period of sixteen years at Londolozi. So although she was born to a completely habituated and peaceful mother, her choice of territory in the rocky, inaccessible terrain of the Tugwaan drainage system meant the game drive vehicles seldom caught sight of her, and because of this she developed an untrusting relationship with people. I have since come to learn that leopards have strong individual character traits, so it's possible that she was simply an unusually aggressive animal in her own right.

Whatever the case, the Tugwaan female was an unpredictable and potentially very dangerous leopard. Some days she could be completely calm and accepting, virtually brushing herself up against the vehicle as she moved along and guests would be able to take as many photos of her as they wanted. On other days, she would rush up to the vehicle and try to take a swipe at guests, drivers and trackers alike. She was unpredictable and that's what had always made tracking her on foot so terrifying. And because of this history, I understood why Renias, for the first time in our short association, had asked for the rifle to be brought along.

That my first leopard-tracking experience was to be with the Tugwaan female significantly added to the overall stress I was already suffering from. Even if Renias and I found her on foot and managed to return to the guests safely, there was no guarantee that we would then all be able to view her successfully from the Land Rover. She was also a very evasive leopard and, in fact, that's what makes seeing any wild leopard such a special and unique occasion;

if they don't want to be seen they have the ability, aided by their camouflage, to melt away unseen. Viewing leopards is mostly on their terms.

But that day Renias and I had no choice. No other fresh leopard tracks had been found anywhere else in the reserve that morning. The circumstances Renias and I found ourselves in were also unique as we hadn't actually tracked any animals on foot together. Usually, he would instruct me to take the guests in the Land Rover, drive to a specific road and wait for him there. He would take his handheld radio and follow the tracks he had found into the bush in an attempt to find the animal. I would remain behind in the Land Rover with the guests. While waiting for Renias, I had to entertain the guests by pointing out various trees and birds that I had learnt about only a few months before.

During one drive, the author of a leading South African tree publication was with us and essentially took over the game drive in Renias's absence. She had the other guests enthralled by her vast botanical knowledge and her explanation of plant sex and communication. I, by contrast, had nothing to offer in the presence of this highly informed and impressive expert. Worst of all, I didn't even know who she was.

On numerous occasions, we hosted guests who had been visiting Londolozi for more years than I had been alive, who probably had far more knowledge than me, let alone how many game drives they had been on in comparison to me. Sitting and waiting with the guests meant I had to constantly talk and engage. I was nineteen years old and my ability to entertain and host people was severely lacking. When I considered the difference in age, life experience, influence and wealth of most of our guests, I started to feel socially and intellectually vulnerable and I became increasingly introverted. More importantly, I felt I was missing out on the tracking adventure; learning from one of the last great African wildlife trackers, or so I had been told.

As a way of avoiding awkward exchanges and as a coping mechanism in the early phases of my guiding career, I found it much easier to keep driving as I could then let nature do the talking. But the idea of being a driver guide never sat well with me as I wanted to experience the bushveld more intimately and walking on foot, tracking animals, gave me a sense of unfiltered immersion in nature. It was a place of contentedness for me, the likes of which I had never known before. I loved the sound and feeling of the ancient granitic soil beneath my feet. I loved the apparently random insect activity of beetles, butterflies and grasshoppers peacefully going about their business. I loved walking along the ageless game paths knowing they were created by wild animals centuries before.

So that day, whether by force of the pure circumstances of having to find the Tugwaan female or perhaps there was a far bigger plan we both didn't know we were a part of, when Renias signalled for me to bring the rifle, he was inviting me to track with him. I was bursting with excitement at this prospect and felt for the first time I was being given the chance to act as a true guide. And, in addition, my role on this tracking expedition, I felt, was as the protector. I was the one carrying the .375 Holland & Holland magnum rifle and I was the one who had been through the advanced rifle-handling course with Chris Irwin, a Canadian and ex-French Foreign Legionnaire, who was Londolozi's environmental manager at the time.

Chris Irwin and his experience were formidable. I found him incredibly intimidating and, at times, I feared him. He was tall, physically strong and wiry with dark, narrow-set eyes that stared at you like an eagle. Both his wrists were tattooed with 'bangles' that resembled military rank rather than a bracelet for beautification. No one ever knew what these tattoos meant and those who did ask were told it had nothing to do with them. Chris was mysterious and not even his long-time neighbour at Londolozi knew much about him.

His rifle training was legendary and intense. He left little to chance, starting with the history of weapons, the mechanisation, through to human psychology, rifle safety and ultimately ending with the trainee shooting hundreds of shots into moving targets from compromising positions on the shooting range. If he felt you were in any way careless, he had the ability to deliver the most forceful and articulate tirade, the likes of which I doubt I will ever hear again. I witnessed several trainee guides visibly shaking in their boots at the hands of his instruction.

Most trainees who failed the guides' programme failed because of the weapons part of the course that Chris was in charge of. Those who did pass the course did so with much pride and skill knowing they had developed detailed knowledge and sound competence in the safety and handling of a high-calibre rifle under pressure.

A few years later I formed a meaningful friendship with Chris and he became the most loyal and honest friend. Chris guided me through many challenges in my early career and I owe that most enigmatic of men a lot for his support.

On Renias's instruction that day, I took the rifle out of the vehicle and walked towards him. We left our Canadian guests in the Land Rover and started to follow the trail of the leopard. Safety in the bush among wild animals is derived from awareness, not from a weapon. Renias told me many times in those early years that although we must legally carry a rifle, it is our eyes and ears that would keep us safe. In order to follow that trail, Renias needed to look at the tracks on the ground. My job was to look up, so that in the event of us finding the Tugwaan female, I would hopefully spot her at a safe distance before she became aware of our presence. That was the theory at least. The tracks headed downstream in the sand in a south-easterly direction. The Tugwaan donga was surrounded by very tall overhanging ebony trees that provided lots of shade, and the riverbed banks were thick with vegetation, offering ample hiding places for leopards. Every so often a half-metre-wide hippo path led away from the donga, used by the animals like highways to traverse and patrol different areas of their respective ranges. We had only gone about 50 or 60 metres when I noticed a subtle change in Renias's body language. Initially, he moved at a casual pace, chomping on a green apple as he tracked. Now, he shoved the apple in his pocket and started to move slower and then muttered that the apple was too noisy to eat. I considered the possibility that he knew something that I didn't and so we kept on. I was making sure that I wasn't missing anything, staring into all the areas of dappled shade. As we progressed, we slowed down, until at one point Renias stopped, knelt down and drew a circle in the sand around one of the tracks. He told me, 'these tracks have walked right now' and I quietly giggled to myself at the image of 'tracks walking'! At that moment, about 150 metres down the donga, a tree squirrel started to make an alarm call. Tzrrr-tzrrr-tzrrr. A squirrel's alarm is for snakes, eagles and leopards being in the vicinity, and as we had just seen an African hawk eagle fly overhead we weren't sure if the squirrel was irritated about the eagle or whether the leopard was actually that close. This added to the already significant tension we were feeling.

Renias turned to me and said that if the leopard charged he would come and stand directly behind me and grab hold of my belt and that I should not run. He would essentially control and guide me. I personally didn't think all these theatrics would be necessary; after all I was trained by Chris Irwin in viewing potentially dangerous animals on foot so I was prepared. I wondered whether the leopard could possibly see us where we were standing. We continued at a snail's pace, stopping every few steps to listen. Renias was hardly looking at the tracks any more and was instead focusing on the surrounding vegetation. The tracks were now very distinctive in the soft sand and, for the first time, I could see them clearly. As I knelt down to get a closer look, Renias immediately gripped my shoulder and told me it wasn't the time to crouch down. I stood up and we carried on.

Up ahead there were a few logs in the riverbed that had been washed down by the previous flood and I raised my leg to step over one. As I put my foot down, I heard a low growl, like the idling of a lawnmower. In a split second, the Tugwaan female exploded out of the bush, lunging straight for me! She moved like lightning and, in a flash, she was at my feet. I had no chance to load my rifle or even time to lift it. Thinking her next move would be to pounce on me, I decided to take a few steps backwards. As I attempted my retreat, I tripped over one of the logs and landed on my back; the rifle flung from my reach. This initiated another charge from her and this time she came forward and landed with one paw on the log I had just toppled over. Sand hit me on the shins. I could smell her breath and I was certain she was going to bite me in the throat. I couldn't feel my body and kept waiting for the impact. My mind was so focused on the leopard's movements, I could think of nothing else.

Her tail was lashing from side to side and after what seemed like minutes but was actually a few seconds, I heard Renias say, 'Hey, Majombane, hima.' (Hey, Small Boots, stop.) Well, I definitely wasn't going anywhere as by now she was making mini mock charges at me almost as if she was deciding whether or not to follow through with the attack. I expected the worst and I started to experience an internal struggle where my head told me to stand my ground while my instinct was telling me to take my chance and run. Renias told me not to look her in the eyes and I immediately looked down. This made it more difficult because then I couldn't see her and her growling had become deafening. Like someone was revving the lawnmower.

Renias told me to move back very slowly and, as I started to move, I noticed a subtle break in the leopard's aggression; something had changed. It was almost as if she'd decided to let me off this time and, in no position to negotiate, I continued to drag myself painstakingly backwards on my bum without making any sudden moves. The leopard started to relax and eventually, when I was about 5 metres away, she bounded away, grunting in irritation.

By the time I got up, the sweat was pouring off my face. In an effort to compose myself, I accidentally rubbed sand from my sweaty palms into my eyes and for a few minutes I was completely blinded. Renias found this quite funny and chuckled quietly to himself but I suspect he tempered his urge to laugh loudly as he could see how shocked I was. We walked out of the donga to a nearby waterhole and I washed out my eyes. I had to sit down.

More than the obvious interpretation of a near-death experience, I was struck by the sheer force of energy exhibited by that leopard. It had literally subdued me and I was both petrified and amazed. As the fright slowly drained out of me, it was replaced by a horrible feeling of shame. The reality of my failure began to set in. I was supposed to protect Renias. I was the one responsible for our safety yet I was too useless to even hold onto my rifle let alone make use of it. Sometime later I realised that Renias already had a weapon; his calmness, years of experience and the fact that he'd seen an encounter like that many times before were his protection. He didn't need me there.

Seeing the state I was in, he said to me, 'You didn't run and that's good.' He was happy that I hadn't turned and run as that would probably have caused us both to be in a potentially life-threatening situation. If I'd run it might have caused the leopard to engage us physically. Predators are programmed to identify weakness in their prey, and they prefer it when the prey runs away from them as this suits their hunting style. Predators will avoid a head-on confrontation with prey where there is a risk of injury so, if I had run, I would have presented myself as the ideal target. To not run in the face of a full-blown charge by a leopard is probably one of the most counter-intuitive things I've ever done. Historically, humans did not fair well against the large predators of the time and with 250 000 years of that experience residing deep within my DNA, I was being given one clear message by my body and that was to run! Yet, amazingly, something in Renias's presence that morning made me stay where I was at that crucial moment.

'Ndi rivaleli, mfo,' he apologised, which I thought was strange. Sitting at the edge of the small pan we started to debrief the encounter. He continued to say that he had not taken the time to prepare me for such a confrontation and, in fact, this was his fault, not mine. 'You cannot know animals from papers,' he continued in Shangaan. 'You must track them, find them and spend time with them every day. After some years you will come to know them, and that's how you learn about their behaviour.' This made complete sense to me. The incident with the Tugwaan female made me realise how, up to that point, most of my training had been theoretical and it was time to develop the practical skills of bushcraft. Now was the time to learn to move safely, effortlessly and sensitively among the animals without causing confrontation. I needed to transform myself from being an insensitive and blundering spectator. To achieve this higher level of immersion and awareness of nature, I needed to develop a superior linguistic understanding of the wildlife – the calls, the body language and the subtleties of their behaviour.

Crouched beside that pan we agreed that in the future Renias would take me on every tracking opportunity possible so that I could learn. It was clear to me that tracking was to be the medium through which I would begin to immerse myself into the individual lives of the animals that I shared space and time with at Londolozi. On that fateful morning a more than two-decade-long mentorship began, which has forever changed my life. Renias told me it made him happy to see that I had a desire to learn and with a broad grin he told me not to worry and that he would teach me.

Seeing Renias's competence and support for me that day made me feel I could trust him completely but I realised I had to see that before I could trust him. So many leaders expect that we *should* trust them and that's often not possible. This is true in South Africa and in many other countries, where distrust and suspicion are so much a part of society. Renias demonstrated his trustworthiness to me and that is how you learn respect. Competence breeds trust.

Renias showed exceptional technical ability in not only seeing the faint tracks on the road that day, but also correctly identifying it as a leopard, a female and specifically the Tugwaan female worth following. Had he overlooked any of that detail we might have blundered into the leopard at a greater pace with less awareness and precipitated a far more calamitous outcome.

In one defining moment, I changed my views of Renias. What I had incorrectly interpreted as contempt and nonchalance were, in fact, his calmness and experience. From the moment he woke up that morning, Renias was guided by the signs that day, whether it was a remark by the tractor driver, a faint pug mark on the ground or an alarming squirrel. At no point did he impose himself, be the hero, or try to dominate proceedings. A recent comment by friend, life coach and fellow tracker, Boyd Varty, that 'Renias is in constant creative response to his environment,' perfectly sums up Renias's approach while in the bush. That is a virtue of a great wildlife tracker, but also a lesson that could be applied to ordinary people in their everyday lives.

Walking back towards our Land Rover that day, I noticed that for the first time in three days I had started to calm down. The intensity of my anxiety had inexplicably dissipated. For the first time, I heard the birds calling. I realised that the incessant commentary of my thoughts had gone. For a few brief moments, I detected a sense of presence and alertness that I had not experienced before. Reaching the crest near where the Land Rover was parked, our guests were waiting and I stopped to look back down at the donga. I spotted a hyaena strolling down towards the Tugwaan and I wondered whether it had heard the commotion and was going to investigate. Movement in a thicket on the opposite bank alerted me to three nyala browsing peacefully very close to where we had encountered the leopard and I presumed she must have left the area. This, I thought, must be the state of being I needed to access if I was to become a skilled guide. We were in nature; a wild place that could not be controlled and my responsibility was to gently facilitate and guide people, not to dominate and control every aspect of their experience. I was not responsible for their happiness. Indeed, while I developed my knowledge of the landscape it was clear that there was already more than enough activity happening at every moment to allow my guests to make their connection with this magnificent place. I no longer feared the outcome of this safari or whether the Canadians were going to have a good time or not.

'Hey, Alex! I'm pretty sure a big cat just made a call in the brush down there. I've spent time in the backcountry myself and I would know when I hear something,' pronounced the old man of the family as Renias and I approached the Land Rover. He said it like it was breaking news and of course he was right, but we had already decided not to take the guests to view the Tugwaan female as we could not guarantee their safety. Fortuitously, another guide had managed to track and find a calmer leopard close by, so we took our guests to see that one instead. As we approached that leopard, it stood high on a branch in a marula tree in full view, presenting the Canadians with an exceptional sighting. The sun was now above the horizon and the leopard's coat glowed golden. It was a privilege to witness the sheer pleasure on the guests' faces and they could hardly lift their cameras to take photos, so captivated were they by the leopard's magnificence. To see this iconic animal was the reason they had paid so much and travelled so far. Africa's charismatic wildlife remains its greatest asset and as I saw the awe on the faces of my guests, I made a silent pact that I would dedicate the rest of my life to protecting this most precious resource.

Failing is the winning

Trefoil was a lush and fertile Aberdeen Angus stud cattle farm set beneath the Tsitsikamma mountain range of the Western Cape. The plush seaside resort of Plettenberg Bay is a mere 7 kilometres from what was our family farmhouse when I was growing up. The rolling green pastures were dotted with jet-black cows and my father would meticulously maintain the meadows for the cattle, and in turn the cows were as fat as ticks. The farm is bisected by a small seasonal river that feeds three dams with fresh mountain water. These dams teem with large-mouthed bass and a variety of ducks, geese and aquatic life. The land belonged to my grandfather, who my sister, Missy, and I called Beepa (a nickname we had made up from the words 'big' and 'Pa') but my dad managed the farm for him. As a young boy, the highlight of my year was the annual farmers' day that was occasionally hosted at Trefoil. Looking back, I doubt the farm actually made any money but it was regarded as a model farming operation in the area and was an incredible place in which to grow up. Trefoil became the wallpaper of my life and I've carried its magnificence with me ever since. Whenever life gets too strained, I think back to the playful and joyous years on the farm and my memories centre me.

We lived in a modest log-cabin house on the property with a view of sloping green pastures and a pine forest. My grandparents lived in the 'Big House', which was a short run through the pastures to the east of us. Every afternoon after school, my sister and I would sprint through the long grass to the Big House to go to visit our grandmother, Nana, who loved us dearly. When we were very young she would take us on mini fishing trips down to one of the dams. She was always consistent in her kindness and, for me, particularly significant in her role as an on-site grandmother. I remember in her final months, riddled with cancer, her stumbling around the dam through the undergrowth to bring me a fishing net I needed to land a fish. Missy loved horse riding and when she could not get the horse to do what she wanted, which was often, Nana was always supportive.

Having a strong resemblance to Elizabeth Taylor, Nana was as beautiful on the outside as she was on the inside. In the evenings, she would often drink too many gins; probably to quell the emotional pain that frequently comes with a person of a sensitive nature living with a dominant and controlling person like my Beepa. Nana's sanctuary was her garden, which she retreated to on most days and I would watch her from the dam wall when I was fishing as she moved slowly but deliberately, admiring and tinkering with her plants. I loved Nana very much and when she died a feeling of loneliness overcame me that has never really subsided. Thirty-four years later I can still hear her voice and sometimes, oddly, smell a hint of her perfume. Whenever I drive through a mountain pass, fly in a small aeroplane or get close to dangerous animals on foot, I sense Nana. Her presence became so prominent that I eventually consulted a psychic medium to try to help me understand what her presence actually meant. The answer I received was that Nana was with me in spirit and that I would feel her make contact with a slight tingling sensation on my cheek. The words left me cold and I knew exactly what the medium was referring to. I had felt Nana on my cheek for many years but had never linked the sensation to her presence. To this day, I can feel when Nana is close. A man with Native American ancestry once told me that the more deceased family members you have, the luckier and more protected you are. I like to think Nana sees it the same way.

We grew up happy and content in a near-perfect place. Missy and I would often disappear for hours, sometimes days, on horseback, camping out at night in makeshift teepees that we built in the forest. Sometimes we would become afraid and would return home in the middle of the night, feeling as though we had failed in our mission to survive. We used to pretend we were American Indians as we rode our horses' bareback with feathers in our hair and wielding bows and arrows. When I got a bit older my father gave me an old BSA air rifle. The weapon represented freedom for me; the theory being that I could hunt for my own food and stay out for longer periods of time. As many young children do when learning how to use a weapon, I shot a lot of birds, until one day a teacher told me that I would lose a hair for every bird I killed.

Unfortunately, this didn't stop me and instead I turned my attention to frogs and lizards. When it rained, I'd go on to the veranda and stomp on unsuspecting frogs, a morbid fascination that drove me to squash as many as I could find.

When we went to Nana and Beepa's beach house in Wilderness near George, I would hunt the lizards that crawled up onto the wooden walkway that led down to the beach. And by 'hunt' I mean stalk and squash. Eventually the lizards learnt that I was a dangerous predator and it became a lot more difficult for me to get to them.

One day after a frog-killing session, my mother came outside onto the veranda to discover that I had dispatched some frogs. She looked at the carnage, then at me and told me to sit down next to her. We sat together quietly for a few moments and I was terrified. Usually if Mum got angry she would head for the kitchen to retrieve the wooden spoon for a good hiding, but this time was different and I didn't know how to respond. Gently picking up a dead frog she asked me how I would feel if a giant came and squashed her, Dad, Nana, Beepa and Missy. Animals also have families, she told me. It was a simple message and my first in becoming aware of the lives of others – both animal and human – and a lesson in empathy, perhaps. In her desire for me to achieve wholeness as a little boy, Mum asked that I acknowledge the seriousness of my foolish acts of violence. I did that and made sure I never intentionally killed another creature.

I went to boarding school at Grey Junior School in Port Elizabeth when I was nine years old. My friend from a neighbouring farm, Brett

Clark, and I, actually requested to be sent away to boarding school. We were keen, yet untested, sportsmen and Plettenberg Bay Primary School could not satisfy our fantasy sporting ambitions. I viewed the move as an adventure rather than simply a new school. I valued my independence above all and thought boarding school would be a liberating experience. The high school's 130 years of tradition also excited me. The traditional Grey quad races inspired by *Chariots of Fire*, the Trooping of the Colour ceremony, the Grey Symphonic Winds and Grey's excellent rugby records were all thrilling prospects and I wanted to be involved in all those traditions.

Needless to say, upon my arrival, I was immediately consigned to the Under-11 F rugby team. They told me to play scrum half because I was short in stature and I remember the coach telling me that I was 'high on enthusiasm but low on skill'. During my second practice session, a much larger boy tackled me and sprained my ankle, revealing to me that rivalry on the sports field was hostile. Competition at the boarding house was just as fierce and every morning we had to jostle for hot water in the showers and fight for toast at breakfast. Having grown up in a peaceful home I wasn't accustomed to these constant struggles. If you didn't like someone it was completely acceptable to actually call them to a fist fight 'under the oak tree'. One day I decided to call a boy to the tree who'd been teasing me about having big front teeth; he and I were going to fight it out old style. But I chickened out when he arrived. I was intimidated by his torn-off shirt sleeves and the group of older boys he arrived with, who showed up like a professional fighter's management team! The boy seemed smaller when I had challenged him two days earlier and I no longer wanted to fight him but the other boys didn't care; they wanted to see a fight. When I tried to leave, they caught up with me and dragged me to my rival, who took a few free punches to teach me a lesson for crying wolf.

To survive at Grey I needed to be far more aggressive, and this wasn't my natural inclination. The precocious and often antagonistic ways of the other boys was a challenge for me, on top of which I wasn't accustomed to living constrained by so many rules. It wasn't long before I became desperately homesick. I missed the peace and freedom of the farm and one evening I phoned my parents and told them to come and fetch me.

In the months leading up to my departure for Grey, Mum and Dad had informed us they were getting a divorce. The news was totally unforeseen and with the exception of the odd argument between them over the years, I had presumed they were happily married, but it turns out they weren't. My mother married my dad when she was 22 and voiced a need to 'experience life more fully', not that I'm sure I even knew exactly what that meant at the time. They were both still living at the farm at this stage and would go their separate ways the following year.

They both urged me to stay at boarding school when I called them to come and fetch me that day, a few months later. 'Hang in there, buddy. You will make lifelong friends there,' were my father's words that echoed in my mind, and at the time and under the circumstances, I couldn't see how that was possible.

After my first holiday back at Trefoil, my father took me back to school in his baby-blue BMW 5 series. As we pulled into the car park of the boarding house he got out to unload my luggage and at that moment I slammed the door lever down and locked myself in the car. Dad tried to persuade me to unlock, but I held firm. This was my last chance to make a statement and no words could console or persuade me otherwise. I hated boarding school and saw no reason why I should stay; I wanted to be free on the farm. My father and I were in a stalemate and as I had no intention of unlocking the door, Dad went to go and look for some help. He returned with the housemaster, Mr Clark, a tall distinguished-looking man who played provincial rugby as a lock, and who I quite liked. Although I don't remember the details, they eventually convinced me to unlock the door and Mr Clark reached in to give me a hand. I interpreted the gesture as an overt and direct threat to my freedom and happiness and so I lunged at him. Seeing red and filled with rage, I sank my large front teeth into his forearm, in the same way a caged wild animal would. Mr Clark howled with pain and whipped his arm back. In the end, I was ushered to my dormitory in floods of tears and filled with dread. To his credit, Mr Clark never held a grudge about my attack and I actually developed a connection with him that helped me settle in at boarding school. Eight years later, I matriculated from Grey High School a lot more confident and streetwise and with many lifelong friends. Dad was right.

By the following year, my parents were divorced and my Nana succumbed to cancer, at only 59 years of age, after a short but intense battle with the deadly disease. She'd known for years that she was sick but had decided to keep it to herself. Although I cannot be sure, I believe she looked forward to an early departure from this world; to be free of society's social demands and Beepa's constant intolerance of her soft nature, which he interpreted as weakness. My father left the farm soon after Nana's death and started a new life in Cape Town writing for the *Cape Argus* newspaper, finally realising his love for journalism. He followed a deeply ingrained passion to be creative, which was a complete change in direction, albeit painful, in losing his marriage and having to start over, but one that I believe ultimately enriched his life. Missy and I would travel on the bus to go and visit Dad a few times a year and it was always excruciatingly hard to say goodbye and leave him. To avoid falling into a state of melancholy, I convinced myself that the situation was temporary and this helped somewhat. My mother also moved off the farm and we lived with her in various rented homes in Plettenberg Bay and Knysna, including a run-down old Cape Dutch house on the neighbouring farm called Suikerbossie, which was right next door to Trefoil. It was here that I recall things hitting rock bottom financially. Beepa was paying for our schooling and I don't think my mother was prepared to request any further help from him. He was a severe and stern man and I knew Mum feared him.

I remember one morning asking Mum when we could have breakfast and she replied, 'When the chickens lay their eggs,' and I got the sense she took delight in telling me that. As I got older, and long before the term became popular, it became clear that Mum placed a premium on sustainable living, and she would always ask where 'away' was when anyone said 'throw it away'. Mum grew up in an upper-middle-class farming family north of Pretoria but in her heart she was a hippie. She'd always rejected the traditions of conventional life and I believe her yearning for an alternative lifestyle was realised at Suikerbossie.

Even the basic food items became scarce at Suikerbossie. One morning I shot two white rabbits at the nearby Stromboli's Inn, which got me into a heap of trouble but we ate delicious rabbit soup for several days thereafter.

Mum drove an old clapped-out and badly rusted cream-coloured VW Golf, which had belonged to a local TV installation company and still bore its advertising on the door. To me, that car represented how my family had fallen apart and I despised it so much. Fortunately, most of my friends in Plettenberg Bay didn't recognise us in that Golf but it was worse for Missy, who went to DSG, the fancy all-girls' private school in Grahamstown and she forbade my mother from parking the car anywhere near the school's main entrance for fear of anyone seeing her. I never invited any of my friends to visit me fearing what they might think.

I felt poor and vulnerable for the first time in my life. Growing up, I felt I could ask my parents if I wanted something but now such requests seemed impossible. Missy and I tried as best we could to tread lightly in our home as it quickly became clear that the usual child-like demands, such as asking for new rugby boots, were simply not appropriate. Yet, despite the tumultuous times and our relative lack of money, my mother remained resolute in her efforts to uphold a loving and emotionally supportive environment for my sister and me. She fiercely preserved our core family values of honesty and open-mindedness that we'd grown up with on the farm. Although our time at Suikerbossie didn't quite suit two previously privileged kids like Missy and me, it left us with a heightened awareness of the far greater plight faced by hundreds of millions of less fortunate people in the world. By global standards, we weren't poor.

Three years later, my mother married a South African-born Belgian entrepreneur by the name of Louis Simonis. Louis wore a collared shirt and a cravat every day of the week, even when he was fishing. The story goes that he was a self-made millionaire by the age of 21 by trading in textiles; you name the business and Louis had done it. He was suave, extroverted and confident, he spoke French fluently and spoke it louder with each glass of wine he drank. Just a few years before he met my mum, while in Mauritius, Louis caught what was apparently the 'world record' for a blue marlin weighing in at 648 kilograms. The fish did not qualify for world record recognition because it evidently took two lines at the same time to catch it, which Louis passionately refuted. He maintained that the second line got caught on the marlin's tail for a few brief moments as it swam off. In telling the story, Louis would always chastise the skipper for giving a premature and inaccurate report on the radio, ultimately leading to the fish not qualifying. He carried a photo in his wallet of the fish hanging on a scale and proudly showed it to everyone he met. He once confided to me that he'd tried to release the monster fish but it had been too exhausted and wouldn't have survived. That said, apparently the skipper, who saw the massive size of the fish when it breached, refused to entertain any ideas of releasing the fish.

Louis was a bright and capable man and although Missy didn't like him, I found him interesting and exciting. Initially I found my mum and his relationship to be an odd match considering my mother's alternative tendencies but looking back, it must've been Louis's eccentricity that attracted Mum to him. They had a good relationship, made each other laugh and often travelled to islands in the Indian Ocean in pursuit of business opportunities and they always seemed to be having fun together. Mum loved the adventure, which I suppose she'd always been looking for, and she found that in Louis. However, Louis developed a weakness for alcohol and it eventually became a defining feature of his behaviour. Naturally this caused anxiety for my mother and cracks began to show in their marriage.

A few years later Beepa died. My mother and her sister inherited his wealth, which was apparently reasonably large. By this time Louis and Mum were, among other businesses, running the Featherbed restaurant located in a secluded and serene bay on the Knysna estuary's mouth called The Heads. We lived in a penthouse apartment overlooking the lagoon in Knysna and, for a while, life was good again. I developed a bond with Louis's son, Jerome, my stepbrother, and he ultimately became a great friend and confidante. He was our big brother and together we had fun fishing, boating and skiing and lots of freedom to explore.

It wasn't long before Louis sprung another business idea and this time it was to establish a train that would operate in the picturesque expanses of the Little Karoo. He was also invested in a scheme in the Maldives to re-glaze baths. Quite why the Maldivians more than anybody else needed their baths glazed, I don't know! At one point Louis even offered for me to go and run the company but my father and uncle weren't keen for me to do so. My mother backed Louis in his business ventures by signing surety for some of his projects, but sadly, as the years rolled by, Louis's business prowess began to drown in the copious daily indulgences of wine and gin. More and more I'd hear about increasing debt and other pending deals that never materialised. The more his enterprises tanked, the more liquor he consumed. I remember realising he had a serious drinking problem when I found him sitting in the lounge at 9am wearing a white gown and drinking gin. And as Louis's Gordon's was slowly being depleted, so were the last remnants of financial security my mother inherited from my grandfather.

Eventually, one Saturday morning the local sheriff arrived to attach all our possessions; even our beds were taken. The debt burden had obviously become too large. I was older and so I was less affected by these material losses than I would have been if I was younger. Perhaps the Suikerbossie era had taught me to be comfortable living more frugally. I had developed far more emotional resilience by this time and, if anything, this huge shift in our lives brought Mum, Missy and I closer together. My mum eventually divorced Louis after ten years of marriage and as soon as we could, Missy and I got temporary jobs working in restaurants and bars in an effort to earn our own money. Beepa had given me a single Aberdeen Angus cow, Alexandra, for my sixth birthday, and she bred successfully and provided me with the means to buy my first car, a 1976 VW Golf. Despite our circumstances, Missy and I were mobile and free.

Twenty years later my parents were reunited in a far more interdependent and mature relationship. When I ask Dad his views he said, 'We were too young and irresponsible to make decisions on marriage. But we've always loved each other.' And when I pry further as to why the relationship worked this time round, he says, 'We spent time clarifying our expectations, and resolved that compromise would be a daily event for the rest of our lives.'

Over the years, I'd grown progressively more interested in wildlife and the wilderness. Whenever possible, I would accompany my friends from school to their farms in the Karoo. The open spaces, quietness and the wild animals that occur in that region inspired me. At one point, I wanted to leave school in order to follow a career as a game ranger. There were times when I couldn't think about anything else except for a life in the bush living among wild animals. I read *Jock of the Bushveld* several times and in the end I wrote my own version. My teachers often accused me of not concentrating but I was concentrating, just not on their lesson. Other than history and biology, I found the rest of the subjects at school uninspiring and unnecessary. Beepa noticed my passion for nature and would tell me enthralling stories of his days as a big-game hunter, which I would then embellish and recount to my friends at school. He taught me some basics of bushcraft and suggested that I enrol in a junior professional hunter's course, which I duly did. Beepa and my dad had taught me to shoot clay pigeons when I was younger and I became a reasonably good shot over the years, which ultimately earned me school colours for 'other sports'. Going up to receive my colours blazer during assembly at Grey remains my proudest moment in an otherwise emotionally tumultuous period in my life.

One year Beepa took us to his brother Skattie's farm, Kingsland, in what was then the Eastern Transvaal. Kingsland shared an 11 kilometre east-west stretch of the Crocodile River as an open border with the southern Kruger National Park. The old 1950s farmhouse faced north over the river and had an exceptional view of the magnificent Kruger National Park. Today, Kingsland is a successful community-owned game reserve called Mjejane. Back then the adults would sip their gins and watch the animals drinking in the river below while sitting on the stoep. Mostly cattle but also some sugar cane were farmed on Kingsland and occasionally lions would cross the Crocodile River at night to hunt Skattie's cattle. I once listened to an exasperated Skattie recount how the lions would charge at the cattle kraal and cause the beasts to stampede and break out of their safe haven, making them easy prey even for a young inexperienced lion. Skattie lamented that the culprits were juveniles mostly under three years of age. Usually the lions didn't finish eating the kill before dawn and would return to the safety of the Kruger Park during the day. To me, Kingsland was the ultimate wild place. I remember once going for a walk as a small boy, accompanied by Nana, who pointed out a lion track close to the house. I loved the fact that the lions were nearby and I visualised them walking over the lawn. In the evenings, Beepa and Skattie would delight us all with tales of marauding lions and elephants and I went to sleep every night hearing the hyaenas calling, animals that have always symbolised wildness, and I felt the happiest I'd ever been. I couldn't get enough of the trees, their shapes, the bird calls and the unique smell of the bushveld earth and I was like a child in a toyshop, where there was almost too much to take in. I spent the days with Skattie and Beepa scouting the vast Kingsland area and we flew over the Kruger Park in Skattie's aeroplane, which gave me a sense of the vastness of the area. The thought of millions of acres of wildness below thrilled me. Nothing in the world mattered to me and for the first time in many years, I forgot about my life back home.

With evidence of the lions on Kingsland, Skattie was preparing to lay a trap for them. Looking back, I don't think I stopped to consider what that actually meant at the time. The young lions had killed a calf and Skattie predicted they would be back the following evening to finish off the carcass. A hut constructed from branches was built over the calf, with three different entrances and a steel gin trap. 'They'll be back tonight,' said Skattie.

That evening, I accompanied Beepa and Skattie to investigate the traps. Skattie drove and Beepa sat in the front passenger seat holding a large rifle and I sat in the back next to an African man, a tracker, who sat holding a spotlight. He never uttered a word. Beepa and Skattie chatted to each other and as we got close to the trap-laced hut, we saw eyes shining in the darkness beyond. Yellow eyes blinked quickly in the spotlight and before I could make sense of what was going on, a loud bang rang out and the lioness bolted away, the deafening noise of the shot reverberating in the bakkie's cabin. Composing myself, I looked up. Did Beepa miss? We drove forward a few metres and on closer inspection we saw that two lions were trying to fight themselves loose from the traps. The sound of their desperate growls will never leave me. One of them, more feisty than the other, was biting the steel trap in an attempt to get itself free. When Beepa approached, the lion launched itself at him and was violently yanked back by the chain that was fastened to a tree. Beepa shot both of the lions in quick succession. The experience left me physically nauseous. 'Zandy, did you see which way the lioness went, boy?' asked Skattie. Beepa's first shot hadn't killed her and I had seen her bound off but I told Skattie I hadn't seen anything. By this stage I didn't want to see any more lions die. Beepa called me to join him for a closer look at the two dead lions; one had shat itself and the smell made my nausea worse. The tracker then got out of the vehicle and started to ferret around for evidence of a blood trail, which he quickly found. I suppose Beepa thought it would be educational for me to see a lion close up. The tracker indicated that he wanted to follow the blood trail from the lioness's bleeding chest wound and he walked off into the darkness unarmed. I was concerned for his safety as we were now following a wounded lion. For a while we drove directly behind the tracker until the bush became too thick to continue. Skattie then agreed that it was too dangerous to carry on. The trail headed in the direction of the Crocodile River towards the Kruger Park. The tracker indicated that he would continue to track the lioness at first light the next morning; it appeared he would know where to find her. We returned to the house at midnight.

The experience left me shaken. While I had grown up hunting and fishing, this was different as it was more of an execution than a hunt. It was like capital punishment for an animal simply following its instincts in a quest to stay alive in a world overpopulated by humans. In Skattie's eyes, however, those young lions were akin to dangerous criminals; villains who threatened his very livelihood by eating his precious cows. To some extent I empathised with Skattie but I was more afraid for the lions. I now know, after spending many hours with lions, that those youngsters would in all likelihood have been pushed out of the park by a more dominant pride. They probably had nowhere to go and found the lumbering cows on Kingsland their best chance of survival. Killing two of them seriously jeopardised their chances of success as a future pride where even the loss of one key member can cause total ruin for a pride.

Bouncing home that night in the Toyota Land Cruiser, with the bodies of the two lions on the back of the vehicle, I looked back and experienced a strange bodily anguish that I couldn't shake for a number of hours. I desperately needed to make sense of it all. If every farmer killed every animal competing for space and resources, we would soon decimate Africa's most valuable asset, its wildlife. There has to be a better way, I thought. Thirty years ago I had almost no ability to articulate my emotions and I didn't know whether hunting was right or wrong. I had never heard, nor considered, the pros versus the anti-hunting debates. I'd grown up with hunting on the farm but the fact that one of the most prominent people in my life had just killed two wild lions left me confused. I honestly didn't know whether to praise or condemn Beepa and so I kept quiet. All I knew was that I experienced a physical reaction that wasn't positive and even though I went into the experience very excited, I was left with a feeling that was intense and without adequate description. Although traumatic, it reinforced my desire to follow a career in the wild. I wanted more lions in the world, not fewer. And I wanted them to be free in the wilderness; sadly a romantic and naive view. And hunting? Well, all desire to hunt died with those two lions.

Once I matriculated from Grey, I left home and moved to Johannesburg to study. I lived with my uncle and aunt, Philip and Cathy van den Heever, who've done more for me, on so many levels, than I probably realise. Philip and Cathy absorbed most of my expenses while I was living in Johannesburg and in many ways they facilitated my next phase of life. Once again, I was more interested in the subject of wildlife than in the marketing course I was studying. My family had told me I needed a business qualification to be successful in life so I enrolled at Damelin Business College. But I had other plans. All the game reserves had their head offices situated in Johannesburg so I decided to drop off my CV at as many of them as I could find. Poor Cathy drove me to umpteen places! Having seen John Varty's and Elmon Mhlongo's wildlife documentaries on TV, I was especially keen to go to Londolozi. John and Elmon's partnership reminded me of Dr Ian Player and Magqubu Ntombela, whose friendship, camaraderie and shared experiences tracking wild animals were all very enticing to me. I urgently and anxiously wanted to be in the wild, at Londolozi, to immerse myself in that life, but I was told I was too young. Londolozi preferred their guides to be at least 21 years old. Even though I was only nineteen, there was no way I was going to wait two years to be accepted and I decided to persist. I sent my CV to Londolozi's head office three more times but I received the same response: I was too young. Not deterred, I returned to the Londolozi offices in Sunninghill and offered to work for them for free. I would do anything, I told them. Thinking they wouldn't take someone so young and inexperienced seriously, I also got my father to phone Shan Varty, Londolozi's co-owner, to explain my desire and enthusiasm, 'my passion', as he told Shan. I went to their offices so many times that people who remember me from all those years ago say I 'camped there'! Eventually Shan told me that I needed to write an exam to test my general knowledge of animals and so I virtually abandoned my marketing course to study for the test. Days later she called to say I could accompany the general manager to Londolozi. I never got my test result but I didn't care. I knew that if I actually got to Londolozi I would find a way to prove my worth.

I was known as the 'cadet ranger' at Londolozi, a fancy name for a skivvy. I painted the toilets, transferred luggage to Skukuza airport, set up bush drinks and performed any errand required of me. And I did everything at a pace; I ran between jobs or to collect tools from the workshop. I wanted to make sure management noticed how seriously I took the opportunity and I also knew the quicker I completed a task, the sooner I might get to do something more interesting. After a few months, I was invited to attend the ranger selection course led by Chris Irwin, the soldier-cum-land manager renowned for his intensive rifle-training courses. There were twelve of us jockeying for just two available guiding jobs. We slept in the bush at night and had to complete various physically testing challenges by day, mostly on an empty stomach. On the first morning we set off on a 'birding walk' and were told to take all our books and binoculars. After just 1 kilometre of walking, we were introduced to our 'conscience' – a 10-kilogram sandbag – and I realised the activity was designed to test our endurance rather than our ornithological knowledge. Some 45 kilometres later there were only five of us left on the walk as the hot and humid January day had taken care of the rest. I was buoyed by having completed the walk and felt confident of my prospects of being selected. The hardest part was when we then had to prepare a five-star bush breakfast for the senior guides as we were starving by this stage and the sight and smell of muesli, fruit, bacon and eggs severely tested our resolve. Some of the guys pilfered a few chocolate muffins from the buffet table, which gave them a much-needed boost, and while I was tempted, I didn't want to give anyone any reason to chase me off the course. As far as I was concerned staying hungry was totally worth it.

Finally, on the last day of the course, sitting around John Varty's green pool, we were given the results. Most of us were delirious from lack of sleep and food. The course was cleverly designed to extract your most honest intentions for wanting to become a Londolozi guide and, going into it, I didn't realise how desirable the job was. In the one-on-one sessions with Chris, he interrogated your every response with painstaking patience and detail, to ensure he got to the truth. No doubt his time in the French Foreign Legion assisted him in this regard. Although nerve-wracking at times, I found his techniques to be refreshing – always brutally honest yet respectful at the same time. This was no ordinary interview that you could prepare for and Chris stripped you bare of the usual safe frivolous statements people tend to make in an interview and often get away with. 'I am passionate about nature' is a firm favourite!

By this point there were only four of us who remained as contenders. I'd failed. Apparently I was too inexperienced, lacked knowledge and was too young. Chris must've seen the look of devastation on my face when he told me my attempt hadn't been successful and my first thought was to run away. I reckoned you didn't necessarily need a job to live in the bush. Quite how I thought I would survive living in the bush was unclear! But thankfully Chris had a plan and he offered to allow me to stay on at Londolozi to prepare for the next selection course. Apparently I had an 'auspicious' attitude; I was given a second chance and one I will always be eternally grateful for. Six months later I became a fully fledged trainee guide.

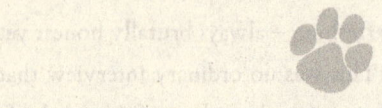

Under an ebony tree

My first encounter with Renias Mhlongo was 25 years ago when I arrived at Londolozi Game Reserve. He was wearing a faded olive-green trench coat and was speaking loudly to another tracker who was standing at the window of the guides' room. As he ambled down the pathway peeling an orange, I approached him.

'Is your name Renias?' I asked.

'Why?' he replied.

'The head ranger says that you will be my tracker when I'm qualified,' I said boldly.

'Ah-ha,' he murmured and kept walking.

'We must go into the bush this afternoon so that we can get to know each other before we start working together,' I continued as I walked faster, trying to keep up with him.

'Is that you talking or the head ranger?' he asked, looking straight ahead.

I later learnt Renias had worked with thirteen different guides before I arrived at Londolozi so his impatience was understandable! Why is this man being such an idiot? I asked myself. Surely if he is my tracker then he is my tracker, finished and klaar.

He disappeared out of sight before I was able to respond. We never went into the bush that afternoon, or any afternoon for the next three months. What I didn't know was that Renias and I would have the rest of our lives to explore the bush together and I just needed to be patient.

Over the years, Renias and the Mhlongo family told me many stories about their beginnings, which I gradually pieced together to get a sense of their history.

According to Renias's South African identity book, he was born on 19 March 1963, but he maintains that his mother simply picked a random date on the calendar. Whatever his true birthdate, Renias was born in a mud hut under an ebony tree in the southern greater Kruger National Park.

Renias's grandfather, Mbezula Mhlongo, lived a semi-nomadic existence and over the years had gradually moved his family westwards from Mozambique, often establishing abodes for a few years at a time before moving on again. At each juncture, he constructed a small homestead where his family lived until their crops stopped producing optimally or the grazing was no longer sufficient for their cattle. 'The land tells you when it's time to move on,' Renias said to me, explaining his family's history, which made me realise how foreign that concept would appear in today's society.

The landscape consisted of a geological area of igneous rock called gabbro, which gives rise to grassland areas of dark, clayey earth called black cotton soil. When it rains, the soil becomes very sticky, making it difficult to traverse on foot and almost completely impassable for vehicles. During the winter months, the soil dries and contracts, causing deep cracks, and this swelling and contracting has an effect on the structure of the vegetation, resulting in a sparser landscape. The black cotton soil is, however, rich in minerals and, when combined with its capacity to hold water, provides good grazing for livestock and is excellent for growing vegetables.

The semi-nomadic lifestyle of the Shangaan people, which Renias described, promoted a sustainable use of the plants, animals and the soil in which they grew their vegetables. Renias remembers his father lamenting the lack of space that was available in contrast to the freedom that their forebears had enjoyed.

Whenever I ask Renias about his childhood, it doesn't matter where we are or what we're doing, he finds time to regale me with story after story – always with a big smile on his face. When he took me to where the Mhlongos had lived, he showed me where his family used to collect fresh water each day – a mini dambo or small floodplain where water bubbled through pale-coloured clay to the surface all year round. It is easy to see why people would have chosen to settle there for a while, with its parkland landscape, fertile soil, fresh water, abundant animal life and a great vista of vast grasslands dotted with knobthorn and marula trees. Animals such as wildebeest and zebra and large carnivores such as lions, leopards and hyaenas were abundant.

The decimation of wildlife in the area came in the early 1800s with the arrival of colonial hunters who brought with them the idea of commercial harvesting of meat, hides and ivory for profit. There are numerous reliable accounts from early colonial pioneers describing in awe the numbers of animals they discovered in both the highveld and lowveld. By the mid-1800s most of the great herds had already been severely depleted by the onslaught of these European commercial hunters. Indiscriminate shooting of animals beyond individual needs was never the way of the Shangaan people who, at the time, only killed for their own needs. As Renias explained, his family never had the means either to 'mass kill' or store the meat for long periods of time.

Renias and his family call themselves Shangaan, a group strongly associated with the long-established Tsonga ethnic group of South Africa and Mozambique. The Tsonga people originated in Central and East Africa and, while similar in many ways, the Tsonga and Nguni are separate 'Bantu' groups. Theirs was a powerful trading kingdom that bartered fabric, ivory, copper and salt, to the extent that they created trading 'companies' along the Mozambique east coast. The Tsonga ethnic group includes several different groupings, with Shangaan forming a small portion of the larger group. Shangaan people (Machangani) are largely a Xitsonga-speaking group of Ndwandwe (Zulu) origin. Shangaan is not recognised as a true dialect of the Xitsonga language group even though its grammar and vocabulary are remarkably similar. So although sharing an origin, the Shangaan people have their own identity that they fiercely defend.

Renias and his family lived in a homestead consisting of five circular mud huts, a cattle kraal and a goat kraal. One of the huts was used to dry and store maize and the hut walls were constructed from mud collected from termite mounds and reinforced with somewhat termite-resistant knobthorn poles. Red grass was harvested and bundled to create conical thatch roofs. The floor was prepared by mixing cattle droppings, sand from a termite mound and water, and the mixture was then laid down, dried and polished. 'It was always shiny, Buti,' Renias once said to me. The door was constructed from poles cut from a tree called a round-leaf kiaat, which is also readily available in the area.

The family consisted of Renias's father, Judas, and his two wives, sisters Anania and Zotas, and eight siblings – four boys and four girls. Renias is the last born. Renias refers to Anania and Zotas as 'my mothers' and the family was so close that it was only in his early teenage years that Renias realised that Anania was his biological mother.

Judas met his Swazi wives through his older brother, Engine Mhlongo. Engine could be referred to as a subsistence hunter, but in the eyes of the local law enforcement, he was probably regarded as an outright poacher. Engine was a self-confessed hunter, proud of his bush skills, which he used to kill for profit. Engine would leave deposits of salt at various distant locations in the bush, conveniently positioned to cure his meat. When I asked Renias whether he'd learnt a lot from Engine he told me Engine would only hunt alone. 'No one ever knew his tricks,' Renias laughed.

Like many of the Mhlongo men, Engine was charismatic and charming, to the extent that while he was being transported to jail he managed to get the police, who he'd come to know well, drunk, stole their keys and made his escape. Apparently he got his name from his ability to outrun the police if they chased him. Renias told me that he was so confident that he would outsprint the police that he would whistle mockingly, like a steam engine's whistle on a railway line, as he ran away. Engine was arrested for poaching so many times that eventually the authorities gave him a permit to hunt legally!

Engine lived on a platform in a tree with a roof made of zebra skin and it was here that people would visit him and listen to his fascinating stories and purchase fresh meat from him. And it was at his 'house' that Judas first made acquaintance with Anania and Zotas.

The Mhlongos grew various crops that included groundnuts, a type of peanut, beans, maize, sugar cane, chillies, pumpkins and melons. Renias told me that as a young boy he ate many small creatures such as borer beetle grubs, grasshoppers, termites, mice, cane rats, tortoises, scrub hares, bullfrogs, civets, genets, francolins and most of the bird species that come to the ground to feed, such as hornbills, magpie shrikes and starlings. 'We didn't have a fridge to store lots of meat, so we ate small things. And I was never hungry at that time of my life,' recollects Renias.

Occasionally an antelope was slaughtered for the family to eat.

Whenever Renias and his brothers were out with the cattle or goats in the bush, the only things that mattered were to protect the livestock and to find food. Keeping the livestock safe was the priority as losing one would mean they would have to face the wrath of their father. Vulture activity indicated the possible presence of a carcass or predators feeding on a kill, and so the brothers always kept a close eye on any vultures they saw in the vicinity. To this day, Renias is always quick to interpret whether a vulture is descending to a roost or dropping with the intention of landing on a carcass.

The four Mhlongo brothers were known to relieve leopards of their kills while they were feeding and a subtle inconsistency in a tree, such as a faint patch of red (which meant there was meat) or a dangling leg, was possible evidence of a carcass. This is something Renias is particularly attuned to, even at several hundred metres.

On one occasion, while Renias and his brothers played in the clear waters of the river, their herd of goats wandered off unnoticed. On registering their absence, the brothers were immediately struck by the possibility of what was to come. Especially Renias. A year earlier he and his mother had nearly lost Mary, their beloved donkey, to lions while they were on a trip to fetch maize from the local store, 4 or 5 kilometres away, and he was acutely aware of the likelihood of fierce retribution by his father.

'No second chances with our father,' said Renias. Brother Elmon, by contrast, was nonchalant, saying the goats had probably started to make their own way back home. It was getting dark and the young men still had a few kilometres to walk.

On their arrival back home, the brothers discovered an empty kraal with no goats. Judas sent the boys back out and told them not to return unless they had the full complement of goats. During the search that night, the boys chased away a clan of hyaenas only to find two half-eaten goats on the footpath a few hundred metres from the homestead. Renias says he shook with fear as reprisal by his father was inevitable.

Judas lived up to his wrathful reputation by doing something that none of the boys expected; he told them to be seated while he boiled the remaining innards of the two dead goats in a big pot. Everyone sat in silence. When the pot finally boiled, to mete out his punishment, Judas instructed the boys to sit in a row and open their mouths so that he could administer the scorching broth. He started with Elmon, gripping him forcefully by his arm. Judas was a physically powerful man and Elmon started to scream. Fortunately, when they heard the commotion, both Anania and Zotas, who knew Judas's temperament only too well, came running to the boys' rescue and ultimately managed to dissuade Judas from what almost certainly would've resulted in severe injuries for the brothers.

Renias remembers Anania swearing at Judas, which was so culturally shocking that he believes it distracted Judas enough to abandon his punishment. Whether Judas's attempt at punishment was a show or not, Renias says he and his brothers never again lost another cow or goat.

In the days that followed, Renias and Elmon decided that, in an attempt to appease their father, they would hunt a warthog, meat that they knew Judas loved to eat. They spent hours investigating termite mounds excavated by aardvark, in search of fresh evidence of a warthog in residence. Warthogs modify large cavities dug and abandoned by aardvark, which feed on the termites, for safe refuge from predators such as lion and leopard. As soon as the shadows lengthen in the late afternoon warthogs make their way back to their burrows, and you seldom find a warthog outside its burrow after dark. The brothers went from mound to mound looking for fresh tracks that could indicate a warthog was inside one of the holes. Just as they were to return home, at a distance, Renias spotted what he believed was a warthog reversing into its burrow. The brothers rushed up, but the animal was already deep inside and out of reach. The sun had already set, and the light was fading quickly, so Elmon suggested they plug the entrance of the burrow with a few sturdy branches, effectively blocking the poor animal's exit.

With delight, Renias ran home ahead and told his father that they had successfully trapped a 'big' warthog in its burrow. Judas was equally enthusiastic but suggested they deal with the animal the following morning, saying to Renias in Shangaan, 'You have worked well, my boy,' words he knew to be particularly complimentary coming from his father. The next day the men rose extra early, before it was light, taking a spear and a long pole with them. Judas instructed Renias to gather a tight bundle of dry grass that he attached to the end of the pole, which Elmon lit. Judas carefully removed the plug of branches and Elmon inserted the 'fire pole' deep into the burrow in an attempt to smoke out the unsuspecting pig. Judas stood off slightly to the side of the entrance ready with his spear, in full knowledge that if the warthog collided with him, he could be severely injured by its razor-sharp tusks. Smoke began to billow out of the burrow and Renias wondered how much smoulder the warthog could cope with. He looked at his father, who by this stage had clearly expected the warthog to appear. But there was nothing. Judas changed his position to get a better look inside the burrow when, like lightning, a honey badger exploded from the entrance, producing a loud shrill scream.

The tenacious animal launched itself straight at Judas, who also produced a high-pitched scream, covered his groin and shouted 'voetsek', while running off into the woodland. The legend goes that honey badgers protect themselves by attacking the soft groin area and genitalia of their attacker, something Judas appeared to have heard about! The brothers simply could not hold themselves together and also ran off into the bush to rid themselves of laughter so as not to be seen by Judas. Renias told me that while Judas was not amused at the time, he eventually saw the humour and went on to recount that story many times over in his life.

Tracking animals was a deeply entrenched daily practice of the Mhlongo family. The men would start reading the tracks as soon as they woke; whether it was noticing a mice trail near their maize store, checking the ladies' direction to fetch water or following the trail of an injured cow. The Mhlongos tracked every day, so much so that I believe they formed a subconscious tracking mentality that has extended to many parts of their lives, in that everything is investigated and little goes unnoticed. Renias remembers his first solo tracking experience one morning after a thunderous evening of pouring rain. He ventured out to see what he could find and not too far from the homestead he found a set of scrub hare tracks neatly preserved in the mud from the previous night. The rainstorm had provided a perfect blank canvas, reflecting only the most recent animal activity in great detail.

The budding tracker immediately recognised the opportunity and, almost as if he was attached to an invisible string, he felt an energy pull him forward to pursue the little animal. This was Renias's debut lone tracking mission and being without his brothers or father made it even more exciting. Renias followed the hare's trail meticulously for about an hour, seeing where it had fed on the wet stem of a shrub, then where it briefly rested and then where it meandered towards a patch of short grass. The tracks often went in circles as the hare returned to the same plant more than once to feed. He discovered that it joined up with another hare and then he followed both of them, noticing how much quicker he could move on the trail of two hares. For the first time in his life he became completely immersed in the life of a wild animal and he experienced an energetic connection, sensing that he and the hares had become intertwined.

'I wasn't thinking of anything else, and I don't know how long I was there,' he says, indicating that he'd potentially fallen into a meditative state. He then came across the track of a jackal – competition and evidence of another predator pursuing the same hares. For a while he lost the trail as the hares sprinted for survival. He then saw claw and skid marks, revealing how the hares had desperately managed to outmanoeuvre the jackal. Eventually the jackal gave up; obviously too much energy expenditure for too little reward. Renias felt for the jackal in the same way he could feel his own hunger but he was also strangely relieved that the hares had escaped. After the encounter with the jackal, the hare tracks showed that they returned to their usual bounding gait, moving slowly and feeding on grass as they went.

Renias resumed the trail but the tracks were sometimes difficult to follow because of sudden changes in direction. As the day warmed up Renias gradually started to feel fatigue as he wasn't yet used to the mental focus required to track an animal successfully. But just as he was about to abandon the trail, the hares' tracks disappeared into a little thicket and didn't re-emerge, which told Renias they were right there. 'I didn't need to kill the hares because my body was already filled with energy, so I left,' he says.

Beyond the practice of following animal tracks, Renias developed an ear for bird calls, especially their alarm calls, which he used to good effect. He learnt to mimic their calls and soon Judas noticed this uniqueness about his youngest son and, in fact, nurtured it, eventually teaching him how to call in greater honeyguide birds and follow them to the beehives. This is a fascinating human-animal relationship that has developed in most parts of Africa where humans and honeyguides co-exist. The bird literally produces a specific repetitive chattering call indicating that it intends to guide a person to a beehive. Honeyguides will deliberately lead human honey-hunters directly to bee colonies, so that they can feast on the leftover grubs and beeswax. Following honeyguides to beehives is quite common and has been widely studied, but calling-in the bird so that it starts to guide the person to the honey is only practised in very remote places. As a young boy, Renias mastered this technique, which eventually became his channel of emotional connection to his father.

Late one blustery afternoon a cheetah chased down and killed a steenbok close to the Mhlongo homestead. Judas was resting in the shade watching his cattle and, having heard the commotion and the bleating sounds of the dying antelope, he decided to take a detour to investigate. In the half-light, he spotted the predator standing over its freshly killed quarry. Since cheetah don't pose much of a physical threat to humans, which Judas knew, he simply ambled up and hustled the cheetah off the steenbok and took the meat. Renias remembers they had not eaten fresh meat for some time so the sight of his father returning home with the steenbok draped over his shoulder felt like Christmas for the family. The Mhlongos feasted that night, complete with copious amounts of marula beer.

Two days later the police paid a routine visit to Judas's village and discovered the steenbok's salted and curing skin. Although Judas tried to explain that a cheetah had killed the animal, the police were not interested. Apparently Judas had not followed the recognised procedure of marking the closest tree with a knife as proof of having found the dead animal. It was an honesty system that, I am told, all the Shangaan people followed religiously. I had presumed you could kill any animal, by any means and then mark a tree, but apparently it did not work that way. That evening, in the fading light, Judas had been in a rush to get his cattle home and he simply forgot to mark the tree, thereby setting himself up as a suspect poacher.

By then it was the 1960s and things were changing in South Africa. 'Homelands' or reservations were being established by the apartheid government and the Shangaan people of the region were being resettled to an identified 'homeland', which would come to be known as Gazankulu. The apartheid ideology decreed that the Shangaan people be given independent and self-governing status. Although the Shangaan people apparently requested their own 'homeland', they were unsuccessful and were therefore grouped together with the Tsonga people, meaning that Tsonga-Shangaan names are used loosely and interchangeably, which today can cause offence. Furthermore, Shangaan is not an official language in South Africa but shares some likeness with, and borrows some vocabulary from, isiZulu.

It was at this time that the Mhlongo brothers, now in their early twenties, came to realise that the freedom of their semi-nomadic lifestyle was drawing to a close and that the apartheid legislation in the form of the Group Areas Act, which effectively assigned racial groups to specific residential sections, was coming into force. The family was forced to relocate to a new semi-permanent homestead that had been set aside in the homeland of Gazankulu at a place known as Dixie.

Life in Dixie was difficult as they were forced to live with people they didn't know or trust. Many of the elders fell into a deep state of depression and often used alcohol to prop themselves up emotionally, causing untold complications for the families. The children, by contrast, were mostly happy playing with the other kids in the village, and Renias met his best friend, Patson Sithole, in Dixie. Their parents had to leave Dixie to find work, which meant the children had to fend for themselves. It was a challenging time as the older siblings monopolised most of the available food, so Renias and Patson began operating as a team where survival was the name of the game.

Renias says the early days in Dixie were the poorest he can remember, to the extent that kids would routinely boil water to drink in an effort to stave off their pangs of hunger. The sandy soil in Dixie held water poorly so cultivating vegetables became difficult and there was far less grass during the winter months, resulting in the cattle falling ill and often dying.

Once, many years later, standing at a huge buffet in Sun City after we'd done a presentation, Renias shook his head and said, 'Buti, so much food here. People don't know what it's like to be really hungry. Dixie made me appreciate food ... maybe too much!'

On the positive side, however, Dixie had access to a reasonably large piece of bushveld that Renias, his brothers and father would slip away to for hours, doing what the Mhlongos do best: tracking.

Welcome to Dixie

'Buti, please come and visit me at my home in Dixie,' requested Renias, late one evening while sitting around the fire in the boma at Londolozi. By this time, we had known each other about two years and Renias's request caught me a little off guard. I wasn't sure I actually wanted to go to Dixie. Growing up on a farm, all the families worked together but we lived and socialised separately. We only went to the black staff's homestead if there was trouble or to attend a funeral, and there was never any 'mingling'. There was an unquestioning acceptance of the status quo and I remember Beepa constantly telling us the 'swart gevaar', the 'black danger', was imminent. I don't recall being specifically warned but Beepa's voice always took on a severe tone whenever he spoke about the supposed threat that black people posed to whites.

When I was ten years old, I experienced the country's apartheid system first hand while on a beach in Plettenberg Bay. Walking through the car park towards Lookout Beach one Sunday afternoon, my mother confronted a policeman who had stopped two

Malawian men from walking onto the sand. My mother ignored the cops' instructions and offered for the men to join us; a decision that nearly landed her in the local prison for the night. I witnessed my mother's absolute indignation at the country's laws as there was nothing she could do, and for the first time I saw her frustration and anger. She was seething, and witnessing her reaction to the police that day had an impact on me. Mum didn't get angry like that very often so I knew something was very wrong and I remember the Malawians' perplexed faces as they wandered off. I don't think they'd spent much time in South Africa and it was probably their first encounter with the laws of the country. 'White' beaches were officially off limits for black people and as a ten-year-old that seemed odd to me.

That wasn't the first time my mum had challenged the system though. As a student in Durban she was caught dancing with an Indian friend at an underground club one night and spent the evening arguing her case with the local security police. Although I doubt she would have been afraid of a night in jail, she was terrified of the repercussions from the severely traditional Beepa. When I asked my mother what exactly she feared about Beepa she said, 'He was a very conservative man and he would have probably cut off the funding of my education.' On another occasion she was chased by three young white men after mingling with black and Indian friends on the beach. That night she feared for her life as she hid in a dingy block of flats while listening to the drunken bigots stumble around trying to find her.

One Saturday afternoon a year or two after the incident on the beach, I watched my gentle and mild-tempered father leave the farmhouse with his pistol stuffed into the back of his jeans to sort out an issue at the workers' quarters. I was stunned and for the first time I considered there might have been some truth to what Beepa had been saying about the 'swart gevaar'. I had heard terrible stories about how dangerous it was for a white person to go into a black person's village and have vivid memories of watching the protests on TV when the government began its policy of 'total onslaught' to subdue rioting in the black residential areas, often known simply as 'locations'. Images of armoured cars racing through the smoke of burning tyres and people retaliating by throwing rocks have stayed with me all these years. One night at school, our housemaster warned us that the 'blacks' were 'pushing back the police' and that we may need to leave. That night I lay under my 'CPA' – or Cape Provincial Administration – sheets terrified and confused about what I should believe.

Sitting around the fire all those years later when Renias invited me to spend a weekend with him in Dixie, I felt no need to give him an immediate or even a positive answer. Dixie didn't strike me as a place I would want to visit, nor did it fit in with my idea of becoming a game ranger and experiencing life in the bush. To be honest, I was only thinking of the most plausible excuse to decline that I could come up with. Periodically, Renias brought up the idea of me visiting his home and I manoeuvred the conversation in another direction, avoiding having to answer.

This went on for about six months and I started to get the sense that Renias was observing my diversion tactics. One afternoon, he commented how beautiful his house was going to look after he installed a new handmade iron gate around his yard. 'It is so beautiful, I wish you will see it one day', he said casually. So with a growing sense of shame for not acting sooner, I decided I would go to Dixie. It was clear that it meant a lot to Renias for me to meet his family, to see his home and to understand his life beyond tracking leopards and lions for wealthy guests at work.

In contrast to the racial divisions I experienced while growing up on the farm, life at Londolozi was so easy. Everyone, black and white, seemed to get along well. We spent our lives telling stories, joking around, playing soccer and touch rugby and, of course, trying to find animals for our guests. This shared experience gave meaning to the relationships we had with each other at the lodge. Most people working at Londolozi were there because they loved animals and people, not to mention the need to earn a livelihood, especially the local Shangaan staff who mostly came from poor backgrounds. The Shangaan people usually stayed in their jobs for many years while the white staff were mostly transient, working for three or four years before moving back to their home cities. There were, of course, exceptions; those who had made a lifelong career working at Londolozi and many of the senior management and experienced guides had been there for a decade or two. Londolozi has a proud record of staff turnover, with some people having worked there for more than 40 years. This level of service and commitment made it different from most other game lodges as the shared common purpose created a sense of unity amongst the staff. One of Londolozi's most powerful marketing tools is the people who have worked there and who have gone out into the world and become ambassadors, often bringing guests back with them to stay.

Having spent most of my adult life at Londolozi, I witnessed a conscientious and highly motivated group of guides, trackers, butlers, maintenance and camp staff who all worked and played hard to make the guests' dreams a reality. Londolozi is the preferred lodge to be employed at, to such an extent that staff from neighbouring lodges regularly jump ship at a moment's notice to work there. During an appointment with the one and only doctor in Skukuza one day, he asked me if I worked at Londolozi and when I answered, 'Yes, how did you know?' he replied, 'I can see you're one of the happy ones.' This was significant considering the Skukuza doctor saw most of the staff working in the southern Kruger Park and the surrounding private reserves.

While pondering Renias's invitation, I started to wonder whether life at Londolozi could be a realistic symbol for multicultural harmony *outside* the high wire fences, in places like Dixie. Considering our country's past, I questioned how deep and authentic the average black/white relationship was. Whenever I left Londolozi to go on leave, it became evident that the relationships I experienced at work were unique and sadly not indicative of the rest of the country and I realised that my knowing Renias only in the context of working together was probably superficial. Going to Dixie was therefore not just morally the right thing to do, but an important socially enlightening one if I was to build a genuine relationship with a man from another culture and from vastly different life circumstances.

CHANGING A LEOPARD'S SPOTS

Dixie is a rural African village the roots of which are deeply intertwined with the apartheid government's rule – an urban attempt to socially engineer, manage and regulate the development and behaviour of the people who the politicians feared most. Many Shangaan- and Tsonga-speaking people who lived in partnership with nature, scattered in small family groups throughout the current-day greater Kruger National Park, were forced to live cheek by jowl in ecologically questionable areas. When I visited Dixie for the first time, there were only about 500 people living there. There was no electricity or running water and people collected wood to cook their food and to heat themselves. The area was so small and marginal that eventually wood became difficult to find and those who could afford to, used gas and paraffin. There was only one operational borehole with a tap and Renias's family had to walk more than a kilometre to fetch fresh water. His wife and daughter used a wheelbarrow to transport two or three 25-litre canisters every few days. As Renias was able to provide more for his family, he bought a small bakkie that made it far easier to collect the water. And as in any town, the affluence of its people can be judged by the architecture and size of the homes. Many of the Dixie residents lived in mud huts with grass-thatched roofs. Since Renias had had a permanent job for about ten years by this point, he was considered one of the wealthier members of the Dixie community, and he lived in a neat cement-brick home with a simple zinc roof and a red steel door.

It was a Friday afternoon, months after Renias's first invitation, that I made my way from Londolozi to Dixie in my baby-blue VW Golf. What should have been a three-hour journey took most of the day as the map Renias had drawn me was about as helpful as the Nando's receipt lying on the seat next to me. I could not make head or tail of it as it showed only one road coming from the Newington gate when, in fact, there were dozens! None of the roads was paved, none reflected on my map and all were in varying states of serious disrepair. In some places, far more road surface area was occupied by potholes than by tar. How, I reflected, had Renias lived with these roads for 35 years? For me it was something of a novelty driving those bumpy roads through the picturesque rural villages, but Renias had had to regularly endure that long and jarring journey over the years. A route that took its toll on his car that fell into a serious state of disrepair – a 'skorrel korrel' – he once said when describing his car, the local slang used to describe a banged-up old vehicle. In comparison, only my newly installed free-flow exhaust system took a beating and I left Dixie with a car that had quite a nice growl to it thanks to a local mechanic who helped me put it back together!

On my arrival in Dixie, Renias and his wife Constance immediately ushered me inside the house to get settled and Renias showed me to his master bedroom. 'This is your bedroom, mfo,' he said gesturing me in. I thought it was a bit odd but he continued, 'This is where you are sleeping. In my room. You are my VIP guest.' Renias and his wife had given up their personal space for me and I'm not even sure where he and his wife slept that night. I wondered whether *my* family would have moved out of their bedroom for someone from another culture who they'd only known for a relatively short period of time. I doubt it.

I will never forget what the bedroom looked like. There was

a king-size bed covered with a bright red bedspread with gold tassels around the edges and a white cloth banner with the words, 'I love you' on it. I'm not sure if that message was meant for me! The headboard had Cape Dutch-like gables, lights on the sides and a built-in radio in the centre. Renias told me he had saved for six years for that bed and headboard and I was overwhelmed by the effort he and his wife had gone to in order to make me feel comfortable. There was a picture on the wall of Claudia Schiffer that read 'My Darling' and the bedroom was in complete contrast to the rest of the home, which was very basic.

When supper time arrived, I expected standard pap and marogo for dinner but instead I discovered that Renias had arranged for Dumi Ndlovu, the chef from Londolozi, who lived in Dixie and was on leave at the time, to come to his home and prepare our meals. This was not a night for pap – we ate gourmet style! Many years later, Dumi went on to win a televised cook-off in South Africa against an Australian master chef champion. Along with the exceptional food that night, the evening was laced with enthralling stories that told of the colour and vibrancy of life in Dixie. After dinner, we sat around the fire and spoke late into the night.

I sat quietly trying to follow the conversation in Shangaan as I'd learnt to speak a bit of the language by then. A man arrived a little later who was apparently Renias's uncle, who asked for a beer and then sat in the shadows. When I asked Renias who he was, he told me his name was Mzinyathi and rumour had it that he lived in a termite mound in the bush. When I asked why he didn't live in the village, Renias explained that the government had offered him a RDP house but he had turned it down, preferring to live in the wild. I watched the man for a while and thought about how I would do living in a hole in an ant heap. Living wild has always attracted me but sharing a residence with the possibility of mambas and other dangerous creatures would not have been my first choice of abode.

More interesting for me was that Mzinyathi possessed the uncanny ability to accurately recall all the poignant milestone dates in his life and of those around him, as well as important dates in political history, all without any formal education. To demonstrate his ability, Renias started to test Mzinyathi's memory and asked him various questions. What date did the Kruger Park put up the western fence? When did Renias start working as a tracker? When was Mandela released? Mzinyathi answered all the questions correctly.

Renias then launched into a story that had me in stitches and for the first time I witnessed the thespian in him. 'When I was a young umfana there was a man here called Kongota,' he started in part English, part Shangaan. He went on to tell us that Kongota owned a small group of cows that he grazed on the land owned by the Dixie community. Over the years, Kongota lost several cattle to marauding lions that broke out of the neighbouring game reserve but on this particular occasion, he had set a wire snare at one of the dead half-eaten cows and managed to trap a single lioness. Apparently Kongota had a keen fondness for booze and Renias said he couldn't remember ever seeing him sober. Having spent most of previous evening at a local bar and with a severe hangover and probably still drunk, the following morning Kongota gathered together as many people as he could muster to help him, grabbed his spear and stumbled off to deal with the culprit caught in the snare. He found the enraged animal desperately trying to shake itself loose and when anyone approached it, it growled explosively, lashed out and would then be yanked back violently by the wire snare. Sensing there was going to be action that day, Renias climbed a marula tree to watch the events unfold from a safe vantage point. Kongota proceeded to mock the lioness by throwing all manner of profanity at the poor animal, smirking in the glory of having finally caught the lion. He advanced to spear the lioness but as he lunged forward in the final act to dispatch it, the lioness retaliated with a new level of aggression and power and in so doing, snapped the wire trap. Kongota, usually a Shangaan-speaking man, instantly started to speak isiZulu and shouted, 'Uh iphukile!' It's broken! He turned and started to run, drunkenly swerving from side to side, frantically mimicking a scrub hare running away from a jackal. But the lioness honed in on Kongota and went straight after him. She caught up to him in an instant and ankle-tapped him, causing Kongota to become airborne. The lioness stormed up to Kongota as he hit the ground and sunk its canines into his buttocks. Kongota skidded along the ground, face first in the sand with the lioness latched on, all the while pretending to be dead. By now people were running around like chickens, shouting and screaming and ultimately unnerving the lioness, causing her to let go of Kongota. She casually jogged off in the direction of the game reserve and Kongota, still shamming death but sensing the lion was moving away, slowly lifted his head and shouted, 'Come back! Finish me!' When the lioness turned to look back at him, Kongota snapped his head back down and played dead again! Miraculously,

Kongota survived the attack but three months later he left Dixie citing evil black magic as the reason the lioness bit him that day.

Renias told the story in broken English, which in itself contributed to the hilarity of the story, but also at great speed, faster with each swig of marula beer as his audience erupted in waves of laughter. He has since told that story to many audiences, and while I've heard it over and over again, it becomes funnier every time and I am told that Renias plays Kongota's character perfectly.

I was to learn in the coming years that Renias's mimicry is one of the reasons he is such a great animal tracker, and strangely also a major factor in the creation of an exceptional life and journey we were to have together. Fast-forward twelve years after that night in Dixie and Renias and I had accumulated many, many stories sitting around the campfire at the 'mecca' of storytelling, Londolozi. We had so many memories together and it prompted us to begin sharing those stories with a wider audience. Before we knew it, we had an agent representing us and we started conducting corporate presentations for big companies centred around our stories.

This was at a time when there was little to suggest that we would succeed and when very few speakers were dealing with the issues of diversity and inclusiveness in South Africa. We have now conducted the presentation all over the world and I am still amazed at how Renias manages to extract humour from the simplest of tales and, just like he did with Kongota, his ability to mischievously imitate the sounds, the voices and mannerisms of people and animals is an incredible gift. He is somehow able to become that person or animal and it is made even more credible and real if he speaks in Shangaan. It's a unique combination of his acute observational skills together with genuine empathy shown for his subject.

One of our first presentations was to an audience of 1 000 people and, as we walked onto the stage, Renias glanced at me and we both knew we were worlds away from our moments around the fire in the boma at Londolozi. Renias is always the highlight of the presentation for the audience, so much so that he once arrived late to a corporate presentation, and with only ten minutes left, he still stole the show! I have watched people shed tears at his family story and similarly I've watched people cry with tears of joy at his excruciatingly funny tales. As speakers, Renias and I were lucky to be mentored by one of the great storytellers, Ian Thomas, a legendary guide at Londolozi during the 1970s and 1980s, and one of South Africa's top-performing motivational speakers for the past three decades. We were fortunate beneficiaries of Ian's generosity of spirit and his trademark focus in helping us to become better presenters. Through much introspection and lots of uncomfortable practice sessions, Ian made us believe that our little story could, and should, be heard by the world.

I woke up the next morning in Dixie to the sound of chickens scurrying around the yard outside. As I peered through my window, I saw Constance attempting to catch one and as she lumbered back and forth, I immediately got the feeling the chickens knew they were safe. To be fair, Constance was no sprinter so she shouted for Nature, her and Renias's six-year-old son, as another fowl easily sidestepped her, to help her grab one. With incredible ease, Nature jogged slowly behind a chicken and swept it up in his hands. It was obvious that this was not the first time he'd caught a chicken for Constance.

Klang-klang! Suddenly there was a loud bang on my bedroom door and when I opened the door, Renias was standing there asking if I wanted to bath. Although he had a bathtub installed in his house there was no running water and I thought to myself that perhaps the plumbing was fitted with the hope and expectation that the government would someday bring piped water to Dixie. After responding that I would like to bath, about 45 minutes later, Nature and his nine-year-old sister, Angela, burst into my room, staggering under the substantial weight of a large rusty zinc bath filled with hot water. 'Here's your bath,' announced Angela in beautiful English. I stood there dumbfounded, staring at the zinc tub and before getting in I contemplated the effort that had gone into preparing it for me.

Angela and Nature had gone into the bush and collected the wood, they made a fire and then went to the borehole to fetch the water with their wheelbarrow. Then they heated what I estimated to be about twenty kettle loads of piping hot water on the fire. I thought about how quickly they would have to have worked as the water was still piping hot when they brought it to my room. The children then brought me a blue 25-litre canister of cold water so that I could adjust the temperature of the water. The energy invested in that one bath was profound and it was an example of deliberate and mindful living that often expresses itself in poor or difficult environments.

The average middle-class South African takes for granted the everyday conveniences of warm water for a bath or shower, purified bottled water or food in the form of a pre-cooked chicken from the supermarket. What is completely subconscious for some represents a whole lot of effort and endeavour for most people in our country. And it's exactly that, the unconsciousness of our daily lives, that is causing us to damage our environment and ultimately our own well-being. If we all had to work as hard as Constance, Angela and Nature for our basic daily needs we would never be as wasteful as we are.

To capture that memory and to ensure the lesson was never lost on me, I asked Renias to take a photo of me that day sitting in the zinc bath. I have stayed in a few five-star hotels around the world since my first visit to Dixie, but the spirit of hospitality at Renias's home that weekend remains beyond anything I have ever experienced. It was extreme hospitality and it represented the ultimate form of giving, particularly when you consider the limited means it came from. It didn't cost Renias much money to put together what he did but it meant so much more than any amount of money. His generosity of spirit made him and Constance the ultimate hosts.

Nature, as I was to learn, was a remarkable young boy. His parents were away at work for days at a time, as Constance worked at a citrus farm near Tzaneen, leaving him and Angela to fend largely for themselves. To some degree, Nature's grandmother was responsible for him but she was an old lady and, like his father had been, by the age of six Nature was already expected to look after the cattle in the bush during the day, amongst numerous other chores, including needing to learn how to find food in the bush. Nature was part of a tight-knit group of similar-aged boys who lived in Dixie. But many of them were nowhere near as fortunate as Nature in terms of having a family member close by or a father who had a steady job, and many of them often had to feed, clothe and house themselves, without the support or guidance of their parents. One winter's evening on a subsequent visit to Dixie a year or so later, I observed as one of the boys organised a jersey for one of his friends who was shivering uncontrollably from the cold. I'd seen the same thing happen with food; the group knew how to look after each other. Via their social network, the boys supported each other with everything they had and due to an exceptionally strong sharing ethic, Nature and his friends were almost entirely independent of their parents. I immediately compared Nature's experience with my own. I grew up with none of the material limitations Nature did and although my parents weren't wealthy by any means, they gave me everything I needed to survive. I therefore grew up completely dependent on them and I didn't need the support of the collective at all. Whereas for Nature, the collective was his means of survival.

This was made even clearer for me while sitting on Renias's veranda the morning of my first visit, observing Constance and her children prepare the chicken for lunch. I realised that our culture is deeply pervaded by individualism; an approach totally foreign to the Mhlongos. I wondered whether this was an advantage, particularly when you consider how a society such as mine has taken individualism to the point of discrimination.

Within 48 hours of my first visit, I was completely immersed in the way of life in Dixie. The glaring contrasts to my own family life were obvious and I gained an early insight into the importance of understanding the perspective of rural communities and their role as stakeholders in wildlife conservation. That first visit to Dixie was life-changing for me and it revealed that despite all the history that has gone before us, there exists a genuine desire by ordinary people to share and to forge meaningful relationships across the apparent cultural divide.

I was met with a level of humanness usually cloaked inside the illusions of social status and material wealth, and, most importantly, the fear of 'them' caused by the unknown. Before I visited Dixie, I had lived by a falsely created narrative of what South Africa is to the majority and who that majority actually is. That weekend educated me in a way that has had a lasting effect on me, especially as I was in the early stages of my career and would eventually become a leader of a diverse team of people. Renias was recently asked why he invited me to Dixie. His answer was, 'I invited many of my guides before Alex and no one came. I almost lost my faith in white people. At the end of the day you must be prepared to risk something if you want to deepen your relationship with a person from a culture different to yours.'

It was a risk, we both agree, that was worth taking.

Realising Renias

'This is where they saw the leopard this morning,' I said to Renias and the guests, as I cut the motor of the Land Rover. That morning one of the other guides had found a young female leopard in a thicket feeding on the remains of a young bushbuck carcass. The guide had left the leopard at about 10am, 200 metres west of Taylor's Loop, a small sandy track with great views of the Sand River, deep in a maytenus (a hardy and evergreen tree) thicket. He estimated that she had been there for a day or two.

The Vomba Young Female, as she was known, had just become independent of her mother and she liked the area around Taylor's Loop and the thicket near the Sand River. Renias suggested we first check the road for tracks before venturing into the brush where she was last seen that morning. He wanted to be certain she hadn't left the carcass to drink at a nearby waterhole on the western side of the road. It was hot and we ambled down the road in search of any evidence that might have contradicted the guide's report. After ten minutes of scouting, I suggested we go to where the leopard had been feeding. I was concerned that our guests were baking in the direct sunlight and I didn't want to leave them for too much longer so Renias half-heartedly followed me back to the vehicle. I could see something was bothering him but I decided not to probe because, as far as I was concerned, we had a solid report that the leopard was nearby.

We started driving and I swung the Landy into the bush, off the road, following the other guide's vehicle tracks from earlier that morning. Just as the tyres left the road, Renias shot around and told me to, 'Keep quiet and listen'. He swivelled on his tracker seat and pointed behind us. 'Hima,' he said, instructing me to stop. Renias had taken his job to teach me to speak Shangaan very seriously and so I was reasonably proficient on game drives where I'd learnt the vocabulary associated with communicating in the bush. I still struggled back at camp, though, where a far bigger vocabulary was used across a range of topics.

A tree squirrel had started making an alarm call in the woodland about 80 metres behind us. These diminutive and exceptionally agile rodents belong to a family that includes chipmunks and they constantly race up and down tree branches vocalising and alarming at predators. Renias always listens to them and regularly expounds their importance when looking for leopards. 'Good security,' he says. In other words, if squirrels are silent it usually means the predator isn't nearby. To me their calls all sound the same and I had almost abandoned trying to interpret their constant utterances. Renias, however, can tell with remarkable accuracy the difference between their irritated social or territorial call or whether they are alarming at a leopard, eagle or snake.

I immediately stopped the vehicle and Renias told me, with urgency in his voice, that the leopard was behind us and I needed to turn the vehicle around. I swung it around with ease, enjoying the power steering of the new Land Rover Defender we'd recently been allocated. We started to make our way off the road slowly, in the direction of the squirrel calls. 'Hurry up, the leopard is moving now,' Renias said with absolute certainty and slight irritation in his tone.

'Can you see it?' I asked. He said he couldn't see it but to listen to the squirrel as 'it's telling us the leopard is now moving'. Incredibly, Renias had interpreted a subtle change in the cadence and tone of the squirrel's alarm call and concluded that the leopard was up and on the move. We were now driving in the opposite direction to where the guide had reported seeing the leopard that morning. I wondered how Renias was so certain there was a leopard, let alone that it was moving. 'Go straight towards that very big jackalberry tree,' he instructed. We approached the tree, picking up speed as we went, and were dodging trees while simultaneously trying to keep the guests from being impaled on the long white thorns scraping past the vehicle. Just beyond the jackalberry tree, I stopped the vehicle. No sign of any leopard. Everyone was quiet, scanning in different directions. Although they couldn't understand Shangaan, the guests had picked up on Renias's urgency and there was an air of expectation and excitement. We all sat silently for a moment. Then a guest asked me how we were so sure the squirrel was alarming at a leopard. A question I was hoping they would not ask! Before I could answer, the guest quickly followed up that question with another more cynical one. 'What are we looking for here, a leopard or a squirrel?'

As I started to jabber an answer, Renias whispered, 'There she is,' and then sat back and started fiddling with his binoculars, as the leopard slipped through a small gap in the woodland ahead. The guests were delighted and we eventually caught up with the leopard further on and had a good sighting. We followed her for an hour as she stalked another bushbuck, which eventually saw her and ran off. As Renias had predicted, she then went to drink water and finally circled back to her original kill on the western side of Taylor's Loop, where she was no longer visible.

We headed back to camp for supper in the boma and the guests chatted excitedly about the day's events. The same guest who had asked me the difficult questions earlier on started to joke with Renias and said that Renias could 'speak squirrel'!

In the years that followed, I observed many such examples of Renias's mastery of using the behaviour of other animals and birds as a means of establishing what predators were doing. There were occasions when he would tell me he thought wild dogs had recently passed through an area based purely on the behaviour of a herd of impala. And he would be specific, 'The dogs, Buti, I can see they've been here.'

The most astounding level of expertise I witnessed early in our relationship, and that still remains a highlight, was when Renias heard a group of birds alarming in a bush nearby and asked the guests if they wanted to see a rock python. We had stopped the vehicle and were having a tea break and everyone jumped at the opportunity. Renias casually walked over to the bush, cup of coffee in hand, and after a few minutes of searching, pointed out the large snake. The pitch, cadence and position of the birds calling from a low point on the bush gave Renias the clues he needed to interpret that the predator they were alarming at was a slow-moving python. None of the guests believed that Renias hadn't known the snake was there and they mocked him, saying he knew the snake 'lived' in that bush! We knew that wasn't the case and Renias laughed them off politely.

Many years later, Renias attracted the interest of a professor of ornithology who started to record and test Renias's accuracy in interpreting which predators various birds were alarming at. The results were remarkable and the result of deep and subtle knowledge acquired through a long-time close association with animals and tracking at Londolozi for close to 40 years.

Twenty-something years later and Renias's creativity and ability to think creatively continue to surprise me. There were instances over the years when I had to work with other trackers, like when Renias had to attend to family matters in Dixie and therefore had to leave Londolozi for a few days. Or when guests formally requested him as their preferred tracker but with another guide. I didn't like being without Renias on a game drive because having to deal with a new personality always took me a few days to settle into and I realised how much unspoken communication had developed between us. Renias would listen to my conversations with the guests and to the radio calls that crackled continuously in the background and I didn't need to tell him what the guests wanted to see or what animals had been found. He always knew. Apart from the constant requests by guests, we both understood that leopards always took preference and then rhino, which we loved to track on foot with our guests. Tracking lions was always third on our list of requests from guests, then elephants and lastly, a distant fifth, was buffalo. Unless the guests specifically asked to see buffalo we made little effort to find them. 'Let's leave the buffalo alone,' we would always say to each other, neither of us finding them all that interesting.

Tracking rhino is fun as their tracks mostly appear big and conspicuous enough for the guests to be actively engaged in the tracking process. We found that rhino bulls usually travelled shorter distances so the chances were good that we could catch up with them. And the guests loved it as they got to 'walk in the boots of a tracker' so to speak, and personally experience the ancient skills of tracking. It's a thrilling experience to track, find and then creep up, downwind, behind a termite mound and watch the large grey beast grazing peacefully, totally unaware of our presence. If we did it right and didn't disturb the rhino, we could get as close as 20 metres away from the great beast. Hearing its chewing sounds while it grazed peacefully, unaware of our presence, can only be described as a spiritual experience. The trick is to involve the guests and ensure they were doing some of the actual tracking. Renias is excellent at coaching people on how to see and successfully follow a rhino trail, while at the same time managing to stay on the trail. It can be a particularly challenging task to track an animal, often in difficult conditions, while simultaneously teaching others.

Occasionally we would lose the tracks, which meant our guests had to stand around until we got ourselves back on the trail. We had to pay careful attention to the tracks, the safety aspect and the overall experience we were giving our guests. It could be all-consuming and on some outings I found this to be mentally tiring.

Over time we got better and better and started to get lots of requests from people asking us to take them tracking on foot. This prompted me to approach the general manager of Londolozi to ask if we could take guests on exclusively tracking safaris. He reluctantly agreed as I think he was concerned about the safety factor of guests actively pursuing rhinos, with all the risks associated with being on foot in a big-game area. I understood this and so Renias and I made our pre-walk safety brief for our guests as thorough as possible. We also had a few criteria people had to meet in order to join a tracking safari, which included only taking people who were physically able to walk long distances. To be sure of the suitability of guests, I would ask their guide whether they thought those guests were suitable for tracking on foot, before accepting them. We offered rhino tracking for about six months but after a while we started to miss tracking leopards, so we went back to doing our regular game drives where we had more opportunity to do so. We logged hundreds of hours tracking rhinos over those months and that experience did wonders for my general awareness and tracking skills.

The cumulative effect of working eight hours a day, year in and year out, in close proximity to Renias, created an intuitive and effortless working style where we were in complete sync with each other. There appeared little to be worried about, and a lot to enjoy, and I found myself immersed in a unique and organic process of education that had me completely devoted. Nothing else mattered to me and none of it felt like work. In fact, there were some months where I thought *I* should be paying Londolozi!

More than the efficient means of communication we had developed, I admired Renias's ingenious and varied ability to find animals successfully on a regular basis. I found myself in the slipstream of his ease and confidence in the bush. We became so confident together that we went through a phase where if we sensed the guests were doubting whether we could find a leopard, Renias would place a bet with them that he could find the animal. Not all leopards though, only the ones we knew we had a good chance of finding!

I was the bookmaker and the opening bet was R500. It was a great incentive to get people to pay attention to Renias's exceptional ability in the bush. For a reasonably small amount of money, it was fascinating to observe how people became completely invested in the process of finding animals, instead of being mere observers. The betting system eventually faded away when we realised the guests would pay us no matter the outcome, and this seemed unfair. It was fun while it lasted, though, and certainly focused the minds of everyone in the Land Rover. We also received one or two poor feedback reports from guests who weren't as interested in leopards and therefore probably thought the betting game was a waste of their time. Looking back, I wouldn't advocate young guides betting on animals as it represented a youthful and conceited approach to the safari that isn't within the spirit of being in the bushveld.

Leopards tread incredibly softly on the ground, making it difficult to recognise their tracks on hard substrate. They seldom move in predictable directions and will regularly double back on themselves if they are hunting. If you are skilful and lucky enough to catch up with a leopard on foot, there's no guarantee you'll actually see the animal as they virtually disappear in dappled light. Renias and I had times when we would lose a track only to discover the leopard no more than 5 metres away from us. If leopards think you haven't detected them, they often go to ground, hide and stare intently, watching as you move off. We learnt through experience that if we were following fresh leopard tracks and the tracks suddenly disappeared, there was a very good chance the leopard was close by and probably watching us! Leopards are by far the most challenging animal to track and find, and you need to be technically competent and have an advanced understanding of their habits. To track a leopard for hours and finally find it is one of the most fulfilling and exciting things I've done in my life.

In later years, Renias and I started travelling to other African countries as well as to North and South America and Australia. It had become clear to me, fairly early in our relationship, that Renias had a multidimensional approach to tracking that few others possess. While I know I am biased, I've never encountered another tracker in the world who has the same imaginative and almost intuitive ability that Renias does. His understanding is incredibly subtle and I recall an instance when a blue wildebeest was alarming on a clearing a few hundred metres away from us. We couldn't see the animal but we were out looking for lions that morning. One of the guides had found a leopard in the very same area where the wildebeest was calling, so to me it was logical to infer that the wildebeest had seen the leopard and was alerting to its presence. We stopped to listen for a moment.

'He's seen lions, Buti,' said Renias, referring to the wildebeest. I thought this was unlikely considering there was a leopard nearby and one of the other guides then confirmed my thoughts when they said it was the leopard who'd agitated the wildebeest. A few moments later, a guest spotted a lioness crouching in the grass very close to the wildebeest. Renias turned and congratulated the guest and gave me a brief glance as if to say, 'I told you so.' It turns out that the longer and drawn-out call versus the short nasal grunts of the wildebeest made Renias aware that it was reacting to lions and not a leopard.

On another fortuitous occasion, Renias followed a flock of white-crested helmet-shrikes that were making intermittent bill-snapping calls in alarm. This ultimately helped him find a mother leopard's den site – a sighting that provided unmatched viewing of leopard cubs for several weeks.

Somehow, Renias always has a plan to find an animal, even when the conditions are tough. Author Malcolm Gladwell writes about the magical 10 000-hour rule where, apparently, practising a skill for that number of hours predisposes you to mastery. I've calculated that Renias has spent, at a conservative estimate, double that number of hours tracking animals on foot. His tracker students at the academy we established together each log approximately

1 000 hours of tracking per year of training with him and he's done that training consistently for the last ten years. Add to that the 27 years of tracking experience at Londolozi before he even started training and that's a lot more than 10 000 hours! And this excludes his time as a boy tracking and hunting, where we will never know how many hours he racked up.

On one of our first visits to the United States, Renias and I were invited to take a group of American trackers into the high desert of Cuyama Valley in the Santa Barbara county of California. Most of the area is referred to as 'badlands' due to its ruggedness, extreme temperatures and lack of water; a description that I think has a good ring to it. South Africans call similar terrain 'crags', although the crags we know here are well vegetated but are similarly steep and rugged in their terrain. The badlands of Cuyama were dry, sparsely vegetated and extensively eroded with very steep gullies and slopes. Although the soil was soft and perfect for tracking, the terrain was hard going; we were either climbing on all fours or skidding down a slope on our bums. There were very few flat areas with groves of pine trees dotting the area and black bear, mountain lion, bobcat and a few species of deer were found in the area.

On arrival in Cuyama, it was apparent that our students were very enthusiastic about tracking with us and one of them said, 'I can't wait to see you guys in action, we've been waitin' for you African boys for a long time.' This statement bothered me a little because as excited as Renias and I were to test our skills in a completely new environment and the idea of tracking bears for the first time was a thrilling one, we also knew a lot was expected of us. I felt proud that we were there as professional trackers; there to share our skills with people in a faraway land. For the first time, Renias and I realised the value of tracking outside of finding animals for guests at Londolozi; a skill I'd subconsciously labelled as parochial that no one was particularly interested in outside of our world at Londolozi.

In America there are many intriguing myths about wildlife tracking. There are stories of how some trackers can 'see' silver lines in a forest, apparently lines of energetic evidence of animals that some trackers are able to detect and then follow. Apparently, some trackers don't necessarily need to see the track impressions on the ground and we were told that some trackers could read the animals' feelings and behaviour, in real time, by holding their hand over a track to sense the energy field. We watched as one woman knelt down and closed her eyes to feel the energy in a track.

This seemed far-fetched to me but as we had no experience with this type of tracking, I suppose I can't judge or dispute it. Renias thought it was bizarre at best and charlatan at worst and he took a dim view of this approach. He's never forgotten that 'woman feeling the energy' and to this day he loves to joke that he knows what the leopards are thinking by holding his hand over a track. Although she doesn't know it, that woman's actions have been the source of many jokes as well as interesting discussions over the years.

On that first morning of tracking in the badlands, we headed deep into a 'wash' called Apache Canyon, a dry creek that temporarily fills and flows after enough rain. Not too far up the canyon, Renias spotted a track and asked me in Shangaan what I thought it was. Before I could answer, one of our participants bounded up to us and shouted, 'Bear tracks, man!' My heart sank. We'd never seen a bear, let alone its tracks and our students were showing us things we were meant to be teaching them. The track vaguely resembled a human's footprint and our students were eager for us to start following its trail. In that instant it occurred to me that going to California to teach tracking might have been a big mistake. We knew nothing about bears or how to track them so how on earth had I got us into this situation. We were about to school local American trackers on how to find their own animals; animals we knew little about. Who were the charlatans now?

I immediately went on the offensive with the participant and pretended to know exactly what animal the track belonged to. Renias weighed in saying he thought the animal had passed there the previous evening and that we should follow it. The opening gambit wasn't easy; we immediately lost the bear's trail and it soon became apparent that bears tread very lightly and leave almost no impression to follow, even in good, soft soil. We made little progress, if any, and I began to feel stressed. The tracks then disappeared on slightly crusty sand on top of one of the slopes.

I then realised I was more aware of our students than of the tracking and I started to feel guilty. They had paid a lot of money for our flights and accommodation and, of course, the cost of their time and I felt I was being disingenuous by maintaining the 'teacher' status. I tried to block out my distracting thoughts and instead tried to focus on seeing at least one print. But there was nothing to see. The bear had grown wings and I wasn't sure what to do next.

The students were crowding around us, asking expectant questions, in high-pitched voices, and they were making me uncomfortable. The concept of a difficult away-game in sports came to mind and nothing seemed certain. The soil, the vegetation, the scents and the bear tracks were all utterly unfamiliar. Renias and I had tracked numerous leopards in far more technically challenging conditions at Londolozi, but that hadn't prepared us for bear tracking in America. I couldn't fathom how it could be so much more difficult and the feeling of working under pressure was compounded by the visible expectations of our students, still so excited to see what we could do.

A feeling of loneliness came over me and I longed for the familiarity of Londolozi. We were thousands of miles away from our home, in a place where we had little knowledge or support, and no one was going to help us put together a successful tracking experience in California, and this made us feel vulnerable.

Renias wandered off in one direction and I attempted to cover as much ground as I could in the hope of finding some trace of the bear. From above, we must have looked like a pair of hungry hyaenas searching for a three-week old carcass. We went around and around in circles, up and down the hills, desperately trying to spot just one piece of evidence that might help us form a picture of the bear's movements. We went backwards and forwards, lost the tracks, found them again, only to lose them yet again. Mostly losing them, in all honesty.

My lower back was stiffening and I could hear Renias puffing in the distance. I wasn't surprised to hear him out of breath, considering the gradients we were navigating in comparison to the flatter terrain of Londolozi. Eventually our students, more than likely feeling disillusioned by this point, stood under a tree in the shade as Renias continued to scout around. It was clear they had given up on us and it was the longest day of tracking in my life. I hated every minute of it. We made no progress that day and, more importantly, we had let down our participants. Who knows where that bear went that day but we weren't close to finding it.

That night we climbed into our tent feeling comprehensively beaten and utterly despondent. We lay awake in silence trying to make sense of the day. Lying next to me in our tiny tent, Renias sat up in his sleeping bag and said to me in Shangaan, 'I think I know how we can find that bear.' I immediately retorted and said, 'Couldn't you have told me that earlier?' He went on to explain that he had noticed towards the end of the day that the bear was feeding on two types of berry bushes, juniper and manzanita, plants that our American participants had told us about. He continued, saying he'd also noticed claw marks on a fallen tree and that he believed the bears were walking along the fallen tree trunks looking for food and not over them, as we had first assumed. 'Maybe they were looking for beetle grubs or honey,' I added. Renias ended by saying that he'd also seen tiny black hairs left by a bear on one of the trees and said, 'These things will help us tomorrow.' The following day we woke with a new plan to follow the bears and made sure we were more open to all the evidence, not just the tracks on the ground.

The second morning we led our group on another bear trail feeling far more aware and this time fully cognisant of all the signs around us. We agreed that I would attempt to follow the tracks while Renias concentrated on the rest. We decided to move slower than the previous day, stop more often and try to anticipate the bear's direction with more discernment, using the berry bushes to navigate. The plan worked and we were far more successful that day and, as the days passed, we continued to improve even more. The more bear signs we started to see, the more confident we became and the less focused I was on the students and eventually we began to enjoy the experience. On the last day I snapped a photo of Renias with a bear foraging in the background; an image that I am very proud of.

That trip to America was a humbling one yet vital to the overall development of our tracking careers. Cuyama knocked the stuffing out of our cockiness and it matured us not only as trackers, but as young men seeking to find ourselves through our work. Amid the fear of failure we both were experiencing at the time, Renias remained calm, hyper aware and focused when it counted; he saved that trip for us.

Cuyama taught us that the principles of wildlife tracking, whether it be a leopard or a bear, are the same. Because we didn't have knowledge of the bear's habits or the landscape, we resorted to a desperate attempt to just see the tracks on the ground and straining to spot some trace, instead of broadening our awareness to include all the bits of evidence that would've helped us understand their behaviour quicker. This lesson pertained more to me than Renias.

Upon returning to Londolozi, our efficiency as a tracking team improved dramatically because Cuyama had taught me to engage in the fundamentals of the skill, the essential building blocks I needed to improve my tracking skills. Renias and I were a well-established guide-tracker team but America made it clear to us that if we were to take our tracking skills to a new level of proficiency, we needed to subject ourselves to more challenging tracking conditions more regularly.

Many years later, fellow guide, author and friend, James Hendry, asked if Renias could train his team of guides in basic tracking skills for his live safari broadcast in the northern Sabi Sands Game Reserve. Following their few days together, James was moved to write me a letter about Renias. He beautifully articulates Renias's skill and tracking as a representation of his art and the extract below is testament to Renias's gift.

> *The title of master is bestowed often with scant regard for what it really means — mostly because those bestowing the title do not truly understand what they are witnessing. It is the sort of designation often given by inexperienced practitioners of whatever craft is being revealed …*
>
> *A master is someone with that rare skill (be it speed, musicality, sublime knowledge, etc.) in whose presence you feel both utterly dejected and supremely inspired.*
>
> *I followed a pride of lions with Renias — a true master of his craft in the very ancient craft of tracking. We didn't find the lions because they crossed out of the reserve but for a few hours I marvelled as Renias followed three lionesses through the late summer bush.*

Far more than actually finding the lions or learning how Renias was doing what he was, I just loved watching him work — in the same way that I might enjoy watching a master musician at a concert. The way you might marvel at the skill of an orchestra or a ballerina. Sure, you might wonder about how they do what they do, but at the end of the day you derive pleasure from watching a performance of masterful artistry.

Watching Renias that day, I became increasingly convinced that while I was enjoying the art for the sake of the art, tracking remains a skill with a value beyond delighting an audience. No machine can yet come close to being able to achieve what he can in the field. His interpretation of wilderness is of immense value to nature tourism, anti-poaching and conservation research.

Renias and, you know this I am sure, you through your work, are ensuring that Renias's skills along with those of other tracking masters are not lost with the passing of this generation and I salute you both for that. I trust that you are moulding the ancient craft for application in modern conservation, honed for the preservation of humanity's last wilderness areas. For me, that's the importance of the skill.

And what of the art? Well that's possibly even more important. The art and the performance thereof are a way for expert trackers to connect people to the wilderness — to something beautiful and worth conserving because it's a part of us. In many ways this is what Bruce Springsteen is doing when he performs his art. Music is a part of our humanity. In many ways, people watch The Boss to reconnect with this element of us, an element that, like the wild, makes us whole and is very difficult to find in the modern world.

Lessons from Eric

Ngala Game Reserve is situated in the southern Timbavati bordering the Kruger National Park. This private land was donated to the World Wildlife Fund in 1992 and in turn handed over the management of the reserve to the South African National Parks Trust. It was the largest donation to conservation of its kind in the world at the time and Ngala was the first private game reserve to be incorporated into the Kruger National Park. Its vast land adjoining the Kruger Park wilderness area is a wild and exciting place for both guides and guests and, when you consider its history of the naturally occurring white lions of the area, it is a thrilling prospect for anyone visiting the reserve.

The main Ngala lodge is in a panhandle situated in the very northern extent of the reserve, in a mature mopane woodland. I was sent there twice in my career, once as a young guide and then years later as head ranger. I loved the drier, harsh environment that is a mopane woodland during the winter and while a vibrant population of tree squirrels take advantage of the trees' natural cavities, we often struggled to find the big cats in the northern area of dense mopane. This meant we frequently had to take guests into the game-rich territory of the south to focus our efforts on finding leopards and lions.

The magnificent Timbavati dry riverbed bisects the reserve on a west-to-east axis, and its natural grassy floodplains, diversified with dense thickets and tall evergreen trees growing along the banks, make it a prime game-viewing area to spot predators such as lions, leopards, hyaenas and even African wild dogs. There were relatively few roads on the 15 000 hectares of land, which meant we were often forced to track and find animals on foot. If a guest wanted to see a rhino, for example, we had to spend at least three hours tracking it on foot. It wasn't unusual for a guide to 'lose' his tracker for the entire four-hour-long game drive while the tracker tracked a pride of lions through a vast block of wilderness. Many guides got lost, especially on a cloudy day with reduced visibility, in search of their trackers. A guide once had to fire a few shots with his .458 rifle just to get himself found! On the eve of my departure from Londolozi for my first stint at Ngala, a senior guide warned me, 'The days of the animals being on a silver platter are gone for you, buddy.' This comment actually excited me since I knew we'd have to do more tracking on foot. It was a well-known fact that although the numbers were good at Ngala, the guides had to work hard for their animal sightings. This was an idea that thrilled me as Ngala felt wild to me and it remains one of the best locations for a young guide to develop their bushcraft.

LESSONS FROM ERIC

After a year at Londolozi, Shan, who gave me the opportunity to go to Londolozi in the first place, suggested I gain some experience in the Timbavati and sent me to Ngala to continue my training as a young guide, knowing it would be good for my development. One of the first jobs I was given there was as the driver of the tracking team that was headed up by Eric Mabilane. Eric was a short, powerfully built man who bristled with energy. He spoke quickly and his bright eyes told the story of a man who'd seen the tougher side of life and lived by his wits. Eric was born and grew up in the Timbavati Game Reserve. His father passed away when he was seven years old, leaving his mother and him and his three siblings to fend for themselves. The family descended into extreme poverty and his mother was eventually forced to leave her children to go and find a job. Eric and his siblings were starving and without parents to provide for them, so he started hunting wild animals as a means to feed his family. Eric's initial hunting excursions were mostly unsuccessful but, motivated by constant hunger and through sheer persistence, he began to learn how to effectively track and hunt ground birds and small antelope such as grey duiker. Apparently Eric and his brothers and sister also tried planting vegetables but the elephants and baboons ravaged their crops before they could eat them. Eric recalls hitting rock bottom when they all had to eat were the leaves of a buffalo thorn tree to stave off the hunger. Eric told me he owned a single pair of shorts and one T-shirt and when he washed his clothes, he'd have to sit naked on the riverbank waiting for them to dry in the sun. A highlight for Eric and his siblings one Christmas was when a neighbouring family gave them a loaf of bread. That was Eric's first recollection of eating bread and he told me sincerely, 'I know it's nothing but bread was very delicious and filling for us at that time.'

When he was a bit older, Eric was taken in and mentored by the manager of a small lodge in a private reserve in the area. Through the skills he learnt there, Eric, despite having no education, found his way into the ecotourism industry and was employed as a tracker at various safari lodges in the area. Eric taught himself to speak English and was a true survivor in every sense. He lived like a tracker – following the fresh trail of life wherever it led him and if he felt the trail he was on no longer served him, he simply switched course; hence his history of employment at several lodges.

Although Eric was extroverted and bubbly, he was discerning about people and observed the subtleties of human conduct and body language carefully, in the same way he'd come to master animal behaviour. At his core, Eric was aware, wily and circumspect and I detected a suspiciousness in him that gave me the sense that he'd been let down by someone important at some point in his life. Perhaps this was due to his difficult childhood. In social situations he loved to laugh and dance and responded well to the light-heartedness in people. Like Renias, Eric was a great mimic and he had the ability to identify subtle quirks in people that he usually turned into a joke. People really responded to that and loved his infectious humour and personality.

In the early 1990s, a single lioness appeared on Ngala Game Reserve, thought to be from Manyelethi Game Reserve in the south. She was pale in colour, had dark rings around her eyes and resembled a cartoon of a criminal in a children's book. She arrived with a yellow tag in her ear, like those used for domestic cattle, and the story goes that she regularly broke out of the reserve and killed the neighbouring villagers' cows. Since Dixie shares a border with Manyelethi, I often wondered whether Kongota and the lioness had ever crossed paths! The park's management had on several occasions caught and returned the lioness to the reserve so the reason or circumstances that caused her to move northwards to Ngala are not clear. Perhaps she was hoping for friendlier neighbours.

She eventually joined up with a pride of resident lions that we called the Big Dam pride, which she ultimately led. Her pride grew to over twenty lions and we regularly watched them in dramatic showdowns trying to kill buffalo, a formidable prey, or more accurately, opponent, for any pride of lions. No ordinary pride simply kills a buffalo; it requires a united effort by skilled lionesses who are fearless, physically big and powerful and who are experienced in the tactics involved to isolate one individual from the rest of the herd. Invariably, successful buffalo kills entail a member of the pride being tossed into the air and therefore injuries are common as the buffalo's horns can inflict terrible damage to a lion. Weighing in at 800 kilograms, a large buffalo bull represented high risk but also high return for the lions and meant meat for days for a hungry lion pride. The Big Dam pride was an exciting group of lions to watch and a sighting of them always caused much jostling amongst the guides competing to see them.

Possibly due to her early exchanges with humans where she had been harassed, chased, darted and carted around, the Big Dam pride lioness developed an extremely aggressive nature. This was the Tugwaan female of lions except a lot bigger and, in a strange way, far more cynical. She was an angry lion and none of the trackers would track her alone on foot and few guides would volunteer to go along either. If you tracked and found her on foot she would always charge. Unlike the Tugwaan female leopard, the Big Dam pride lioness never had good days. The best case scenario you could hope for was finding her in a clearing with enough distance and visibility that you could back off quickly if you needed to and leave her alone.

On most occasions she would growl and start jogging towards you, almost like she was playing a game of 'chicken'. With your rifle loaded and prone, you had no option but to stand your ground and hope for the best. Some of the guides had fired warning shots at her in the past and one of them told me that that was the only way to survive a full charge by the Big Dam pride lioness. She regarded any movement, sideways or backwards, as a sign of fear or a threat and it only exacerbated the situation. It seemed anything could turn a jogging growl into a full-blown charge. As my friend, mentor and fellow tracker, Ian Thomas, once said to me, 'Your courage is the first line of defence against this lion.' Just a few weeks before I arrived at Ngala, a tracker had tracked her in thick bush and was nearly killed when she took a swipe at him, tearing his old khaki NATO jacket in the process. She was a dangerous lion and I always assumed she would one day either seriously injure or kill someone.

Eric loved her. 'This is a wide [wild] lion,' he would say to me. This seemed obvious but I felt I needed to listen to him as I sensed 'wild' may have meant something different to him. Eric's modus operandi to track the lioness was at speed until he felt she was close and he'd then leave the tracks in an attempt to find her by approaching from a safer angle. If the tracks were fresh and entered a thicket, he'd break away from the trail, position himself downwind and stalk through the woodland until he got a view of her. On several occasions he told me to hang back and at other times he would climb a tree and use my binoculars to try to spot her; anything to keep her from detecting us.

On one particular occasion while tracking the Big Dam pride with Eric, he lit a large joint and after a few puffs it seemed to make him track even faster. He told me it helped him track better and I suppose it could be similar to artists who claim marijuana boosts their creativity. A few months before, I'd read a book that explained how tracking as an art requires significant creative and divergent thinking so perhaps Eric was onto something.

I was struggling to keep up with a somewhat-stoned Eric that day, let alone see the tracks on the ground. On approaching the southern bank of the Timbavati, we noticed tiny pug marks amongst the adult tracks of the pride; clear evidence of cubs. We'd seen the lioness mating with a large unknown male lion a few months earlier and we'd also seen evidence of her lactating by the wet suckle marks around her teats, so I was sure the marks belonged to her cubs. I immediately voiced my concern to Eric because following the Big Dam pride lioness with her cubs would have been a death wish.

'Then you go back to the Land Rover and wait for me there,' said Eric when I told him I was worried about our safety. I seriously considered abandoning Eric as my sense of anxiety versus the exciting prospect of finding the cubs was playing an enormous emotional joust in my head. Eric clearly backed himself and had often referred to trackers who'd got themselves into precarious situations with the Big Dam lioness as 'mampara trackers'. I stood thinking about what my training had taught me and the possible danger ahead, but in those few seconds, Eric had already disappeared. I was encouraged by his conviction and by the power and clarity he conducted himself with throughout that trail and so, with little time to think it through any longer, my adventurous bulletproof twenty-year-old attitude ultimately came to the fore and I chose to track on with Eric. My fear of what *might* have happened was a distraction and it diverted my attention from the task at hand, probably making me less aware and more vulnerable. My heart was pounding and for a while I lost feeling in my knees. To combat the nervousness, I pushed away any thoughts about what could happen and I actively elected to be 100 per cent all-in with Eric.

We knew the cub tracks were fresh as it was about 11am, and they were on top of an impala herd's tracks that we could see had recently drunk water from a pool in the riverbed. The lions had passed by no more than an hour before. We slowly pressed forward, stopping every minute or two to listen for any evidence, alarm calls, or anything that might have given us an idea of their position. The grass was long and every so often a thought swirled in my mind that if we found the Big Dam pride lioness in that grass we would definitely be charged. I was doing everything against all the training I'd received to date and Hugh Marshall, the head of guides for CCAfrica, who had been instrumental in my training at this point in my career, would have been devastated to know what I was doing.

We carried on and, in his usual cavalier approach, Eric had the rifle slung casually over his shoulder. I wanted to tell him to be more ready with it but I couldn't muster the confidence to say anything. The tracks turned and headed in a westerly direction parallel to the Timbavati and through the riverine thickets. Eric whispered that he thought the pride was looking for a place to hide the cubs and his excitement was palpable. The trackers at Ngala were fiercely competitive and if Eric found the Big Dam pride lioness's cubs, he would have some serious street cred, and he knew it.

The trail led us across a road towards a series of small clearings. 'Is close by,' Eric grinned, referring to the lions. As was his usual strategy, he decided to leave the tracks and approach from the north, downwind from where he predicted the lions were resting. By this stage, the experience had taken on an intense vibrant energy that had me captivated and I wanted to keep following the tracks. But Eric whispered loudly, 'No, boy, let's go.'

By this stage, our every step was made with painstaking effort to avoid stepping on a dry twig or anything that would make a noise and alert the lions to our presence. We were no longer tracking, we were stalking, creeping up on the most dangerous animal I knew. We circumnavigated a large guarri bush that was obscuring our view and as we came around the thicket, we spotted the lions lying in the middle of a small clearing of short grass. We froze. Eric smiled briefly.

The lions were lying about 40 metres away from us with their backs to us. I saw our crazy lioness lying to the left of the pride, much paler in colour than the rest, with two cubs that were playing with her tail. Her head was flat on the sand and she was completely unaware of us. The strong breeze was fortunately blowing in our favour so at that moment the lions had no way of detecting us. Eric signalled with his forefinger for me to reverse. If the lioness saw us, we would be in all manner of trouble and my heart was pounding in my ears. I looked back to find the best route to extract myself quietly and as I took my first step, I felt Eric firmly grip me by the arm. 'Stop,' he said.

I glanced back and he had a stony look on his face and was gesturing towards the lions. I swivelled quietly and gawked ahead; one of the cubs that had been suckling the lioness had climbed onto her back and was watching us. Surely a three-month-old cub wasn't going to sink us now, I thought, and for the first time I really considered that I'd probably made a poor choice to join Eric. We both stood and stared at the cub for a few seconds, neither of us quite sure what to make of the situation.

One vocalisation of alarm from the cub and the mother would have stood up. If she turned, she would have seen us straight away. Whether the cub was planning to notify her mother of our presence we didn't know but we weren't going to hang around to find out. Eric urgently motioned for me to continue backing off as our only hope was to put distance between us and the lioness. We reversed in slow motion for 5 or 6 metres and then a metre or two later, we turned and broke into a jog.

Fortunately, the Big Dam pride lioness never charged us that day, and that evening the guests staying at Ngala were presented with a magnificent view of the entire pride feeding on a giraffe with five small playful cubs.

Notwithstanding the risks that Eric took in the bush, I loved my stint with him at Ngala. It was a privilege to spend one-on-one time with a bush man of his stature; a wild man to his core and a more indomitable person I have not met since. He was impish but he appeared to know the limits, or certainly when I was with him, I think! At the start of my career in the bushveld, my association with Eric was more fulfilling and informative than any 'formal' guide training I had had. And, as with Renias, I never felt Eric was trying to force the learning process on me but was instead putting us in interesting, sometimes testing and stressful situations, which facilitated learning by virtue of his skill. I learnt via 'osmosis' from Eric.

Many years after my first stint at Ngala I returned, this time as the head ranger. It was a leadership role that, on reflection, I probably wasn't fully equipped for. By this stage, Eric had qualified as a guide and he was taking guests on game drives, so our roles were reversed – I was to be Eric's 'boss'. I could see he struggled with this 'boy' giving him instructions, and I tried to be as sensitive as I possibly could in the knowledge that I'd received much from him in a formative, albeit brief, period in my career. He enjoyed advising me when there were guide or tracker issues that needed to be dealt with, and as a 28-year-old I probably had the management skills of a dead buffalo, that is to say, they were non-existent.

Like most inexperienced twenty-something-year-olds, I struggled to manage myself, let alone a team of A-type personalities of guides and trackers, and as a result, I didn't hesitate in taking on a guide or tracker who I thought had transgressed the rules. I was abrasive, naive and immature but Eric taught me the art of listening, a skill that, if I'm honest, I didn't like learning. I could not fathom why it was necessary to talk so much to solve simple staff issues and, to my mind, the person's conduct was either right or wrong. I didn't like the grey areas, mostly because I lacked a whole lot of the life experience needed to recognise what lies between the hard lines of right and wrong. In trackers' meetings, Eric would tell me to listen even when I thought I had listened enough. Those meetings often went on for hours and I sometimes wondered whether we were in fact achieving anything at all. In hindsight, Eric taught me the elusive skill of consultation. It turned out to be an invaluable lesson and it's a skill I am very grateful for.

One morning I received a radio call from Eric instructing me to meet him immediately at the camp in the south of the reserve. By the tone of his voice I could hear something was wrong. I raced to meet him and I found him sitting in his room at the staff village. As I approached him, I noticed his eyes were red and his skin dark and shiny with sweat. He looked furious and I sensed resentment in his anger, which unnerved me. Eric was usually friendly and smiley with an effervescent personality, qualities that made him an excellent guide. He received consistently good guest feedback and his placement at the premier lodge at Ngala was because of his exceptional performance.

As I walked towards the doorway of his room, he growled at me, 'Today I'm leaving Ngala in a box. And you won't do anything.' Recognising that this was no ordinary situation, I simply sat down on the stairs and listened. I'd never been presented with such a statement before and I quickly realised that this was one time

I really needed to listen; more than I'd ever needed to before. But the longer I listened, the less sense Eric seemed to make and after twenty minutes of keeping quiet, I asked Eric what he wanted.

He shook his head vigorously but didn't answer me. I offered for him to take as much leave as he needed to sort out what was going on in his head. I was grasping at straws in an attempt to calm him down. 'No holiday,' he finally said. I asked him if there was someone responsible for his state of mind, if someone had said or done something to him. Again, he didn't answer and so we sat together quietly for another ten minutes. Then the workshop manager, a large burly man, wandered past and this seemingly sparked another tirade from Eric. He shouted and accused the man of being racist, among other things.

'Is this what this is all about?' I asked Eric. In response, he launched into a scathing attack, denouncing various people and events that had played out over the past ten years. Many of the incidents occurred before I had even met him so all I could do was sit and absorb his anger as best I could.

Then he began threatening to take his own life. 'There's no use for me to live anyway,' he said. Realising this was far more a psychological and emotional issue than a work one, I changed my approach. I desperately wanted someone older, someone more experienced to come and help settle Eric, but he only wanted to talk to me. I tried to give him a sense of his value to the world and reminded him of his family and his young children. I tried to reminisce about the many meaningful things he'd done in his life and how far he'd come since the days of sitting on the rocks waiting for his clothes to dry. I talked about the experience of tracking the Big

Dam pride lioness together, but nothing I said changed anything. In fact, I don't think he heard a thing I said and in the meantime he was becoming more and more agitated. He told me his rifle was ready but I'm not sure I really believed him. I was hoping it was a rant that would settle.

Then Eric reached behind the door and took out his .458 calibre rifle. I tried to grab it from him but he threatened to shoot me. In that moment, two cars full of Eric's family pulled into the staff village. The penny then dropped; Eric had already told them of his plans. The situation was very real and this was no rant. This was a man on the edge, preparing to take his life.

I turned to address his family, which in hindsight was a grave mistake. They approached Eric and I with foreboding looks on their faces and behind me I heard the familiar metallic sound of a firearm as Eric loaded the weapon. People were screaming and running in all directions as no one was sure if Eric was intent on shooting other people or himself.

What happened next becomes a blur for me but I remember a loud bang and Eric collapsing to the floor. His family flooded around him, pushing me aside in the process. I sprinted to the office to call an ambulance and while I was on the phone someone told me Eric was dead. The ambulance operator overheard the comment and told me they didn't send an ambulance for someone who was already deceased.

Shaking uncontrollably, I ran back to where Eric's body lay and he'd already been covered by a large grey blanket. I fell to my knees, powerless. He suddenly looked so small and, with all his vibrancy gone, he appeared strangely diminutive. I picked up the rifle and ejected the spent cartridge. There was a lot of confusion as people ran around not sure what was going on, some women were singing and others were just sitting and staring at the events unfolding before them.

Later the police arrived to take a statement; I'm not even sure who called them. Before I could talk to the cops myself someone told them that I had shot Eric. 'Just check the fingerprints on the rifle,' is all I heard. My world, already profoundly shaken, now fell apart at the seams. I was now being accused of murder and it was like my worst nightmare had suddenly become real. Why would someone make such a claim? I then heard another voice announce on the open radio channel that 'Majombane has just killed Eric'. Bad news really does spread like wildfire it seems. This was insanity and I sensed things were unravelling and the police seemed to be far too casual about the situation. Then, as if to rub salt in the wound, a radio call came in to say that a death threat had been posted on the door of my house and that I couldn't go home. Some ignorant person, nowhere near where the incident took place, had taken it upon themself to incite violence and threaten the very person who had had Eric's welfare completely at heart; the one who had tried to stop all of this. How awful this world is, I thought.

Then, like a brief ray of sunshine peeping through dark storm clouds, the village chief came forward and silenced everyone. He told the cops to stop what they were doing, gripped my forearm with his large hand and facing the police said, 'This man was trying to help Eric. He did not touch the rifle before it shot. I was here all time.' It turns out the chief had been watching my entire interaction with Eric so why he hadn't intervened earlier was not clear to me. I was hoping he would follow through by bringing my accuser to book but he didn't.

Nevertheless, the chief had spared me a possible few nights in jail, if not worse, and I was exceptionally grateful for his involvement. I walked away and sat in silence for a few minutes. I immediately began to question whether I had done the right thing and what I could have done differently for Eric. I pondered it as I relived the incident in my mind over and over again. The final moments of Eric's life wouldn't stop replaying in my head, no matter how hard I tried to stop them. In the hours and days that followed, the incident started to affect my ability to even have a simple conversation and I was completely distracted, in a constant state of alarm. That night my girlfriend and I had to sleep in a secret location for fear of retribution by an ignorant opportunist. James Hendry, a work colleague at that stage, was instrumental in providing a coherent and truthful order of events to the Ngala staff, which ultimately had a major effect on calming everyone's emotions. His support for me that day and the courage he displayed in a tense situation became the foundation for a lifelong and deep friendship.

I do not know why Eric took his own life. I have since spoken to many of his family members and friends and no one really knows why he did it. The most common explanation I received was that he was bewitched by someone. A few weeks before his death he'd disappeared into the bush for three days and was found alone, confused, starving, and gave no explanation why he was there. I wished I'd known about that going into the situation, as I may have considered consulting one of the elders of the Shangaan staff to assist me.

Those early days tracking the Big Dam pride with Eric at Ngala will be forever ingrained in my memory. Eric had the rare ability to touch people's lives in such a way that left you with an everlasting sense of profound connection to him. For whatever reason, a deeply personal one, he decided his season was up. For a while I was angry at what he put me through but that faded and I now feel strangely privileged that he called me, along with his family, to say goodbye. A farewell that was incoherent at times and ended in horror but a farewell nonetheless. Sadly, Eric left behind a wife, a ten-year-old son and a daughter who was twelve.

Fifteen years later, Renias and I were interviewing candidates in a village close to Ngala for our tracking school, Tracker Academy. We usually interviewed ten to fifteen people in a session but that day word had spread and some 100 young men showed up with their CVs in the hope of securing a place on the tracking course. We sat for most of the day under a marula tree quizzing each person in an effort to select the final eight candidates. The last interview of the day was with a strapping twenty-year-old man by the name of Raymond Mabilane. He was Eric's son; a spitting image of his dad that I recognised instantly. He greeted me as if he knew me and his big smile and warm persona were all too familiar. It was difficult to see past his father's legacy and I told Renias I was biased and that he should make the final decision. Fortunately, Raymond passed the interview process, giving me the opportunity to close the loop in my relationship with his father. We offered Raymond a bursary to study at Tracker Academy to become a professional tracker; a chance he took with both hands and a prospect his dad would have supported wholeheartedly. One year later, Raymond graduated at the top of his class and is now thriving as one of the most promising young trackers in the Sabi Sands Game Reserve.

It is my belief that sometimes people come into our lives to facilitate certain life lessons. My relationship with Eric was relatively short-lived but its briefness was offset by its intensity in every respect. Eric was a man committed to his truth and principles, regardless of the situation or the consequences. I found that trait to be refreshing and it's a rare one these days. He was a man who was happy to throw caution to the wind and to live with the repercussions. Having grown up hunting francolins for lunch, while other children were eating cheese sandwiches at school, Eric had no choice but to develop a strong sense of purpose in the face of all the obstacles he faced. Eric demonstrated to me how personal power is gained by being uniquely you; by following your own trail despite all the background noise.

Wearing the tag

Looking at me in disbelief, Renias told me to get into the bath. I don't think he ever believed I would get into it on that 42-degree sweltering day in Dixie. This was to be the location for the nhluvulo ceremony I had been invited by the Mhlongo family to participate in as Renias's 'brother', and I had no idea what was to come.

In the Shangaan culture, and indeed in many African cultures, exactly a year after the death of a person, the family and community come together in a ceremony to officially end the mourning period and to celebrate the person's life. This is called 'nhluvulo' in Shangaan.

I had visited Renias in Dixie several times over the five-or-so years we had worked together and I had grown close to his family, especially his mum from whom I learnt a lot about the Shangaan people. The Mhlongos had invited me as a member of their family, a brother of sorts.

I crouched down in the rusty brown zinc bath behind the

cement brick dwelling where Renias's elderly mother, Anania, had once lived. A tall man sporting an oversized pair of blue-tinted aviator sunglasses came around the corner carrying two buckets; one was black and the other was blue. He wore a tatty, ill-fitting pinstriped suit and both the pockets on the jacket were torn and hanging loose. He was wearing a pair of home-made sandals crafted from car-tyre rubber. I couldn't see the man's eyes and it made me slightly uncomfortable because seeing people's eyes tells me a lot about their intentions.

I sensed this man was borderline shifty and I'm not entirely sure why I thought that, but I think it was because I didn't know who he was or what he had come to do. He got closer to me and unleashed a booming monologue in Shangaan, most of which I didn't understand because it was outside the context of a game drive. Every game drive was an intense lesson in Shangaan and Renias was relentless about teaching me to speak the language properly and, quite rightly, refused to speak Fanagalo to me. There were days when I felt frustrated and despondent at my slow progress over the few years I had been learning Shangaan, but one morning, listening to Renias chatting about our plans for the day, I suddenly realised I could understand most of what he'd said. But I still needed to learn the language in other settings such as Dixie, where everyone spoke Shangaan very quickly and used a large vocabulary.

I then felt the warm innards of a goat draining over my head and down my chest as the man poured the contents of the two buckets over me. Bits of slimy green, partially digested vegetation covered most of my torso and the stench reminded me of the unique, unpleasant odour of the internal gases released when lions first tear open the abdomen of their prey. It reminded me of when a Brazilian guest sitting on the back of the Land Rover vomited when the wind changed direction while viewing lions feeding on a kill; the older the meat and the warmer the day, the worse the smell.

This goat had been freshly slaughtered so the smell wasn't too bad and as I had had lots of exposure to predators killing and eating their carcasses, I had grown somewhat accustomed to the smell. But the proximity of the fetid entrails was far more overpowering than I expected. Once the buckets were empty, aviator man said something in Shangaan that initiated beautiful singing from the women who were seated around the front of the homestead.

Renias's mother had passed away exactly one year before and this ceremony was in commemoration of her. No one knew exactly how old Anania was but I was told she was born on the same day as Nelson Mandela, which would've made her around 90 years of age when she died. Renias was the last born and was very close to his mother, so this was an important day for him.

I always loved to watch Anania's reaction when Renias and I went to visit her as her eyes would shine from her lined, weathered, yet beautiful face, that without any words, told a story of hard service, humour and trauma all rolled into one. Anania saw the humour in most things and she liked to tease Renias. Her laughter made Renias happy and I always noticed a lightness and positivity in his disposition after a few hours spent with his mother.

A few years earlier, I'd bought Anania a base and mattress to replace the reed mat that she had slept on her whole life. I thought I'd given her a special gift, only to discover that soon after receiving it, she had donated it to a local children's home, preferring her mat. She told me that sleeping on a simple mat on a hard floor kept her spine strong. Her physical strength was perhaps testament to that after witnessing, on many occasions, her carrying heavy knobthorn wood collected from the bush, on her head, and then taking it back to the homestead.

Anania only visited Londolozi once in the four decades that her sons worked there. I invited her to stay and made sure she was in one of the most luxurious suites. While she loved the experience, she was concerned a crocodile was hiding in the private plunge pool and wanted me to get in the pool to prove there weren't any!

Anania was a powerful woman and Renias always commented that it was her who kept the family together when they moved to Dixie and, years later, when Renias's father, Judas, passed away. Renias often voiced his concerns that when she passed away, the family centre would no longer hold.

A year before, Renias and I had been training trackers at Phinda Game Reserve in KwaZulu-Natal when we got word that Anania had died unexpectedly. I tried my best to console my friend as he fell to the floor, powerless, his cellphone smashing onto the concrete. This big, imposing man wept inconsolably and appeared to have suffered a heart attack as he lay motionless on the floor, unable to speak.

The loss of his mother had a profound effect on Renias's life as it forced him into a provider and leadership role that has taken a great toll. On some of his weekends off, Renias elected not to go home to Dixie, often citing his need for a break from his family as the reason but in reality it was to save money. If a person is reasonably well off and owns a car in the community, they can become the subject of many requests and favours from friends and family members. Added to this was the fact that Renias also helped and supported the local trackers, making for constant demands on his time and money.

I'm always astonished at how many times Renias's phone rings when we travel together; a constant flood of people seeking his benevolence. Few white South Africans understand the obligations and responsibilities of the breadwinners in the black African community to provide financial and logistical support, not only to their immediate family but also to their friends. It is a burden that usually leaves the person with very little money at the end of each month and is often referred to as 'black tax' in South Africa. Irrespective of the amount of money Renias earns each month, he doesn't have much left over once he's settled everyone's requests. The tentacles of support spread far and wide for Renias and sometimes, frustratingly, with little acknowledgement or thanks from the beneficiaries.

The family had lost their matriarch, who had for many years maintained a strong sense of morality and respectability in the Mhlongo clan, and like the loss of the oldest lead female elephant, they were emotionally and psychologically bewildered and disoriented. Since his mother's death, not a month goes by without Renias reminding me to spend meaningful time with my family. Once, while tracking in the Karoo together, he refused to let me fly back to Johannesburg before going to visit my parents in Plettenberg Bay, a three-hour drive away. And to this day, whenever we drive through the Karoo he makes sure we pass by to pay respect, to 'pahla', at an old Van den Heever family gravesite where my great-great-grandfather, Oom Daantjie, is buried.

I went on a family pilgrimage of sorts years ago to assist my uncle Philip in completing the Van den Heever family tree and found some of my ancestors' graves on far-flung Karoo farms in the Colesberg district. Oom Daantjie was the well-known patriarch of my family and I had visited his final resting place in Burgersdorp in the Karoo. It has always been important to Renias that we pay homage to those who have been before.

The nhluvulo ceremony we were taking part in that day is performed by many African groups. 'Kuhluvulo' means to undress oneself and, in this case, the undressing is the end and cleansing of the mourning period. In the year preceding the ceremony the Mhlongo family had asked me to wear a black tag on the arm of my shirt as an indication that I was mourning Anania's death. I was amazed at the latitude I was afforded by, for example, security guards, many of whom are Shangaan and Venda people, when I was in Johannesburg and when they saw me wearing the tag. On one visit to the head office of a company in Sandton, I was ushered through the security checks like a diplomat, such is the respect people have for those in mourning. Petrol attendants, airline staff, beggars, office clerks and the public in general were constantly offering me their condolences; a touching display of kindness from ordinary South Africans.

The process of nhluvulo means the mourner can actively mourn the death of the person and peacefully purge any hidden emotions with the support of family and community. Judging from the expressions on the faces of everyone gathered that day in Dixie, it looked like a therapeutic exercise. I was drawn to the process and even to everyone staring at me. I was apprehensive at first as I feared the unknown, but being receptive to the liquid on my body brought me a strange feeling of belonging, driven mostly by the strong sense of acceptance I received from everyone in attendance.

I was highly conspicuous because of my skin colour but the Mhlongos went out of their way to ensure I felt part of their family and the ritual. I realised that even in the most foreign circumstances you can still belong, a concept I've always struggled with in my life. Humans have an inherent desire to belong; a need that has mostly escaped me, barring my first few years growing up on the farm. The subtle undercurrent of loneliness I'd experienced most of my adult life suddenly made sense to me and in that remote African village in the strange and foreign situation I was in, I felt a strong sense of belonging. The ceremony was inclusive and without judgement and I no longer considered myself the 'mlungu' merely attending as an observer, as I had sometimes felt on prior visits to Dixie. I belonged.

The louder the women sang, the more intense the feelings pulsating through my body became. The ululation slowly ebbed and I stepped out of the zinc bath and was ushered to the front of the house where my girlfriend and a few other members of the Mhlongo family were sitting on a large reed mat. Only Anania's immediate family were sitting on the mat, along with my girlfriend and I, but being invited as Renias's brother meant I was entitled to sit with them. By this time, hundreds of people had gathered around the house and some had climbed trees to get a better view of the day's events. Several children had leopard-crawled under the crowd of standing adults and lay between their feet watching me intensely.

One shouted, 'Hello Majombane!' My 'small boots' nickname that, despite my 8.5 shoe size, is still not big enough for me to shake that moniker! And, in fact, more people know me as 'Majombane' than they do by my Christian name. I once met a guy in one of the villages who told me he was great friends with a white man known as 'Majombane from Londolozi'. When I told him I was Majombane he said the 'real' Majombane had much smaller boots!

Renias sat down next to me on the mat. He glanced at me and smiled. His tightly curled hair was also full of the olive-coloured slime that had caked on his head. It looked like he'd overdosed on La Pebra's hair gel and we looked at each other and started to giggle. A nhluvulo ceremony is an auspicious occasion and one I felt enormously privileged to be a part of. Elderly men and women then started to come forward with donations; gifts of appreciation for the family who had played an important and supportive role in the life of the old lady. Many of the old lady's possessions were also disbursed to those of us sitting on the mat. Desperately poor people, people who would go to sleep hungry, came forward laying colourful cloth material, shoes, shirts, food and even cash, in front of me. This made me uncomfortable and I wondered to myself how I could accept gifts from people who had so little. Sensing my emotional struggle, Renias leant over and told me that I had no choice but to accept their gifts graciously. He went on to explain that should I refuse, on the basis of the guilt brought on by a privileged life, I would disgrace the family and demonstrate gross disrespect to Anania.

One by one, I thanked all those wonderful souls for their kind and generous offerings, an act of bestowing that would no doubt have put them under tremendous financial pressure for the foreseeable future. All I had to offer them in return was sincere appreciation. I purposefully looked deep into the eyes of each giver with the hope they would somehow sense and feel my immense gratitude.

Leaving the nhluvulo ceremony in Dixie in the early evening, my girlfriend and I drove towards Johannesburg in silence, only the whine of the Land Rover's gearbox was audible as it laboured up the Drakensberg mountains towards the Highveld. As the sun slipped behind a peak, I wondered whether my own family would have shown the same level of generosity and inclusiveness that the Mhlongos had shown to me. Does my family foster a sense of belonging like the Mhlongos, I mused as I reflected on the day.

I grew up in a community that easily judges other people as different, and the distinctive approach I encountered in Dixie that day magnified the tyranny of judgement and its power of separation and segregation that pervades society. The ceremony of nhluvulo promotes compassion, respect and kindness; universal truths vital to any functional community. I had experienced all those values first hand and had been given the opportunity to connect with everyone in Dixie, while at the same time be introspective with myself.

Subconsciously, most of us give in order to get and sometimes we give in order to stay socially relevant. Naively, you could be forgiven for believing the nhluvulo ceremony was an example of complete unconditional giving, but I'm sure the givers that day knew their time to receive would come and more likely so if they were in attendance. Having said that, the givers derived no material benefit by giving to me and would have probably experienced further financial insecurity and poverty as a result of their generosity. Their giving may be viewed as a sign of support and respect for the Mhlongo family but equally important is that it may have been an investment in their future.

The ceremony in Dixie was a rarely seen demonstration of basic humanity, an expression of the inherent capacity humans have to care for each other, and it was brought about by compassion, literally meaning 'to suffer together'. At a time in South Africa when entitlement is rife, when the individual's needs are considered more important than the group's needs, we can all learn from ceremonies like nhluvulo to practise self-sacrifice. Small yet meaningful acts of kindness and compassion have the ability to transcend our prejudices and our experiences of other people as 'them'.

Our close association with technology means that because we communicate more often by digital means, our interactions are in danger of becoming more trivial and less meaningful. No amount of cellphone, WhatsApp or Skype chats could ever replace the raw emotional intentions on display that day in Dixie. And for South Africa to try to start to heal, I believe it wouldn't hurt to hold more ceremony, a powerful way to celebrate the transition to a new order. It allows us to acknowledge the past while also creating a new beginning.

WEARING THE TAG

The stench filled the cabin of the Land Rover that evening and became almost intolerable so we decided to stop and overnight at a small country hotel in the small village of Dullstroom. Most of the hotels and lodges in the area are very exclusive and charge equally exclusive rates and I wondered if I would be able to even afford a night's stay. As I entered the hotel lobby to enquire about a price for the night, I was met by the black African manager who was on duty. After exchanging a few pleasantries, it became clear that he was Shangaan-speaking so in my best Shangaan, I described the events of our day and his eyes lit up. After hearing my story of participating in nhluvulo, all he said, over and over again was, 'This is the first time, the first time that I see a white man do this.' From an apparently uneventful Sunday afternoon in the hotel's reception, with the body language to match, the man rose to his full height and told me that he could, under the circumstances, give us a discounted rate for the night. It was a special end to an extraordinary day.

Life with Renias

In only four years, Renias and I had shared so much. He had welcomed me into his family, treated me like his brother, introduced me to tracking and, in addition, I was learning what it meant to be a better human being. I had been looking for a way to show him my appreciation and while I knew there was no real way I could thank him, I wanted to give him something truly memorable and in stark contrast to anything we had experienced together in the bush. Renias had introduced me to a different world and had facilitated within me a sense of South African-ness that I had not known previously. Life with Renias taught me that being South African wasn't only about braais, rugby, golf and visits to the game reserve during the holidays. With a 300-year history of my family living in South Africa, I had a deep-seated desire to understand what it truly meant to be African even though I have a white skin. In all honesty, before I met Renias I had very little understanding of what it meant to be South African, by the majority of the population's standards.

Growing up, I hoped I'd meet a famous business mogul who would agree to be my mentor. I thought I needed someone highly educated and connected who could guide me as to how to be successful and get ahead in life. I'd always loved the bush, but I had many interests and I wanted to carve out a unique life for myself, one that included a range of endeavours. My time spent living in rural parts of the country and with the Mhlongo family had ignited within me the desire to be a social entrepreneur.

I've always recognised the power of business as a force for good and I wanted to provide commercial solutions that could improve people's lives on a material level. This need slowly grew as I got older because my father's approach to raising a son was to leave me be, to let me work it out on my own. A quiet man, Dad gave me the space to test my place in the world, without any predefined views of how life should be lived. As a child I asked too many questions about different topics and my dad's standard answer was, 'They have their methods, Zanda', a nickname only he calls me. His response left me with little option of finding the answers other than to find them out on my own. Although it was subtle, his method facilitated a resourceful approach to life that no university could have taught and both my sister, Missy, and I, benefitted from it.

When I left home at eighteen and went to live with my dad's brother, Philip van den Heever, in Johannesburg, he in many ways fulfilled my need for a mentor. Philip is a big man with a big heart and is bright, witty and an experienced business operator who I'm fortunate to say has guided me like a son. Philip and my father are the most ethical people I know and if I take a business idea or scheme to Philip, the first thing he checks are the values behind the idea.

Renias has been my mentor on so many levels, both professionally and personally, and he made it possible for me to learn about nature through wildlife tracking. Along with learning about the habits of countless animals. I received a scholarship in human behaviour too, since humans are a part of the natural order. Contrary to the approach of a traditional mentor, Renias didn't 'tell' me anything; his invaluable teachings came from observing him move seamlessly in nature and, of course, from his stories.

The opportunity to do something meaningful for Renias came when a friend of mine invited me to visit her in London. I immediately knew it was the adventure I had been looking for and I decided to ask Renias to come with me for two weeks to England. At that stage, he had never been to Johannesburg, let alone London, and he had never flown in an aircraft or seen the sea. I put the idea to him, presuming he would jump at it, but I was mistaken. In the same way I had offered excuses about going to Dixie, the shoe was on the other foot and it was now Renias's turn to journey into the unknown. He finally agreed, saying half seriously, half joking: 'Only if we can drive there.' I explained that the flight would take about eleven hours and we would be cooped up in a metal tube, along with 300 strangers, for the whole night. But I then mentioned that the beer and food was free and this definitely piqued his interest somewhat. I wasn't exactly a seasoned traveller either, with my first visit to London only a few years earlier when I visited an English girlfriend I had at the time. The way I saw it, going to London with my friend was not only a form of exchange in some way but also an exciting adventure for me. The thought of experiencing the Western culture capital of the world with Renias was a thrilling one for me.

We flew on Virgin Atlantic and, to give Renias some insight, I explained how Richard Branson had disrupted the British airline industry by starting his own airline, Virgin Atlantic. I was struck by Renias's immediate curiosity in Virgin as a brand and while waiting for our flight to board, he asked many questions and was keen to experience Virgin first hand after what I had shared with him. I think Virgin was the only airline at the time to offer individual TVs for passengers in Economy Class and I knew this would be something Renias would enjoy.

We boarded the plane, took our seats and as the plane hurtled down the runway, Renias grabbed my leg with his left hand and his seat with his right hand, seemingly in an attempt to hold up the aeroplane. He turned his head to one side, closed his eyes and clenched his jaw so tight that I could see the veins in his neck popping out. He was terrified. Once we were airborne and the seat belt lights were switched off, I ordered us a beer and before long he started to relax and enjoy the flight. At one point he asked an air hostess if she was sure there was enough fuel to get to London! Despite my constant assurances of the great safety record of long-haul flights, Renias was untrusting but he eventually settled and started to peruse the movie channels on his TV. I noticed, however, that with all the choices of movies to watch he settled on the digital map of Africa, showing the breadcrumb trail of the plane as it made its way painstakingly slowly up the African continent. I casually suggested he should watch *Die Hard*, one of the featured films

I thought would appeal to his sense of adventure, but he wasn't interested and I eventually fell asleep. When I woke up, Renias was still watching the map. For the duration of the flight he was glued to the frustratingly slow progress of our plane flying up Africa towards the United Kingdom. He looked at me and said he'd been 'on watch' the whole night just in case something went wrong. When I asked him what his plan was if there was a problem, he sighed and said, 'Not sure, mfo ... wake you up,' with a grim look on his face. Bleary-eyed and on the final approach into Heathrow, he then turned to me and said, 'Buti, if we need to come back here by road or walking, I know the way!' A passenger seated next to us heard the comment and laughed good-naturedly.

It took Renias many years to grow fully accustomed to flying, especially in small planes. Strangely, a turning point in his fear of flying came when he saw a woman getting sick while we were in a small aircraft flying over the Maasai Mara in Kenya. It made him finally realise that lots of people were afraid of flying and he seemed to lose some of his fear. He did continue, though, for many years, to ask the air hostesses on long-haul flights to double-check with the pilot that we had enough fuel for the flight; an earnest concern that he knew always made me laugh.

On arrival that morning at Heathrow, Renias went completely quiet. I could see he wasn't afraid – just intensely observant. While standing in the immigration queue to get our passports stamped,

I noticed how he scanned the room carefully and turned to look back at the people standing behind us several times. Knowing how strict customs officials can be, especially in first-world countries, I prepared him for their possible questions. I needn't have bothered; he sailed through the questioning and left the woman giggling in her glass booth. I don't know what he said to her but whatever it was got him through immigration quicker than anyone else.

We caught a train to central London and eventually emerged from what we started to call 'the warthog burrow' – the London Underground. The sheer number of people pacing the streets with intent and speed was overwhelming and mesmerising at the same time. We tried to walk side by side, like we always did in the bush, but soon realised that it was impossible on a busy London sidewalk. It seemed we were the only ones who had to do all the dodging while the rest of London simply walked in lines like robots. 'They can see we are not from here,' said Renias and, as if in protest, he dawdled along the pavement paying little attention to the oncoming foot traffic. I kept losing him in the crowd, making navigation all the more challenging. The more I told him to move faster, the slower he appeared to walk.

To this day, nothing has changed; I still struggle to get Renias to move at my pace through airports and in cities. He ambles along, staring at advertising boards and stopping to chat to anyone who appears to be open to a conversation. I, by contrast, pick my route and do not deviate from it. A few years after our first trip to London, we nearly missed our flight from San Francisco to New York because Renias decided to explain South African history to a random passenger in the airport toilets. I once overheard him say to his wife, Constance, that if she ever travelled with us she'd better exercise and be fit in order to keep up with me. Renias's ability to live life in the moment has its downside, though. I've always been the one to take care of the details and make sure he's on time and I have developed a real sense of resentment at certain points for always having to be the responsible one.

Whenever this emotion arises, I work to actively reconcile it with the knowledge of how much Renias brings to our partnership in areas where I am totally inept. As a team we have vastly different skills that make us strong together, but our differences also bring with them the challenge of having to constantly remind yourself, often when you don't necessarily want to remember, of the unique contributions brought by the other person. This is something that still doesn't come naturally to me and I have to work hard at it.

In Dixie, people amble along while casually chatting to each other and you only walk briskly or run if it is absolutely necessary. But in London the majority of people seemed to have an intense focused look on their faces as they strode along, giving the impression they were perpetually late for an important meeting. Renias, by contrast, believes that if you are too focused for too long, you will get sick and has said to me, 'You must rest, mfo,' thousands of times over the years. I've always respected his Zen-like attitude and the ease with which he is able to find mindful awareness in the present moment, even in stressful situations.

When Renias was a young boy, one of his interests was motor cars, particularly fast sports cars. While we were on that trip to

London, he asked me to take him to see some of the prestigious cars he'd always dreamt about. So we headed to downtown London to visit a famous dealership called HR Owen in the exclusive area of Kensington. As we entered the dealership, a salesman came forward to greet us. As he approached, I sensed he probably doubted, quite rightly, our creditworthiness. Thinking fast, I told him that Renias was the prince of the Shangaan people in South Africa and we were looking for an estate car. The salesman paused and stared at us for a few moments, slowly nodding his head in an attempt to buy some time to work us out. Renias was wearing an oversized cream-coloured coat that my uncle Philip had given him for the trip, and while he looked reasonably smart, he wasn't dressed in quite the attire you would expect of a HR Owen client. Or Shangaan royalty for that matter!

Still doubting us but now having been confronted with the possibility of royalty, the salesman changed his approach and started to take us seriously. He ushered Renias to a brand-new red Ferrari that was parked in the centre of the dealership and offered for him to take the car for a test drive. Renias got into the driver's seat and before the salesman realised we weren't who we said we were and told us to leave, I snapped a photograph of Renias at the wheel! I promptly turned down the offer for him to drive a brand-new Ferrari down the Kings Road!

With the guidance of my childhood friend, Matt, over the next few days Renias and I visited Big Ben, Westminster Abbey and many of the wonderful historical sites that London is famous for. These trips were interspersed with visits to many of London's pubs where we sampled the local brews. Too many one night when we caught the Underground in the wrong direction, only to discover it had been the last train of the evening.

We spent most of the night walking back to Kate's house where we were staying, and finally arrived home tired and drunk. We started knocking loudly on the door when we realised we didn't have a key. She wasn't amused and left us to suffer for a while out in the cold. Thinking she wasn't going to oblige, I decided to take matters into my own hands and climbed the drainpipe to her bedroom window. In the process, I slipped and dislodged a pot plant that came crashing down onto Renias and onto Kate's brand-new BMW that was parked on the street. Wilful damage of property is probably a crime in England, I thought to myself. I was looking down at the car, hanging onto the drainpipe, and Renias started stammering that we 'needed to leave right away'. He said things would only get worse the next morning when Kate saw what we had done and he strongly recommended we give her time to 'cool off'.

Fortunately, Kate sort of saw the humour in the situation the next day and her Beemer, much to Renias's and my relief, amazingly did not suffer much damage. For the rest of the trip, Renias maintained that we needed to behave ourselves for fear of being thrown out of London. When he said, 'London', I think he meant Kate's house. I'm sure he had done a quick conversion of the value of the British pound to the South African rand when he bought a beer, and was acutely aware that we could never have afforded to stay in a hotel if Kate had asked us to leave.

In the same way I had sat around the fire in Dixie with Renias and his family and learnt about his culture, he had metaphorically speaking sat around the fire with me in London and learnt about

Western culture. By the time we arrived back in South Africa, I noticed he had stopped calling me 'Majombane' and started to ramp up his lessons in teaching me to speak Shangaan, regularly telling me that I must 'speak it deeply'. It is now a language I can speak reasonably well and it has helped me significantly throughout the country, particularly with the traffic police in Hazyview, the town not far from Londolozi. The cops would usually wave me over for exceeding the ridiculously slow 60-kilometre-per-hour speed limit in the middle of nowhere, and I always greeted them in perfect Shangaan, complete with the appropriate tone and accent. They would then either forget why they had stopped me or find it more interesting to talk to a white man who could speak their language. Some would even call their colleagues to come and join the conversation just so they could also hear this 'mlungu' speaking Shangaan. On one occasion, another driver was pulled over at the same time and she became so irritated at having to wait while the cops and I chatted that she drove off!

Whatever the reason, we usually ended up in full conversation discussing things like the heat, whether they thought there was enough grass for the cows to eat and where I worked. If that diversion didn't work, I would ask them if they knew Renias Mhlongo of Dixie, and many of them did. Sometimes these chats could go on for a good ten minutes.

To be honest, I feel a bit ashamed about how many traffic fines I've managed to escape using my command of the language. But my Shangaan charm doesn't always work, as Boyd and I found out when we encountered a Mozambican immigration official at the Lebombo border control. He threatened us with instant incarceration if I continued my antics of trying to charm him in Shangaan. He didn't like the fact that I could speak Shangaan. A few years later, on a work trip to London, Renias and I were chatting to each other in Shangaan in Harrods, when a young man walked past staring. I think he was trying to decipher what language we were speaking, and so intent was he on listening in, that he became disorientated and walked into a display stand of toys, causing Renias to roar with laughter.

In a more urgent situation late one Friday afternoon, I desperately needed to get a temporary passport from the Home Affairs office in Randburg in Johannesburg. The place was heaving with people and my heart sank at the thought of joining the long, snaking queue knowing I would never make my flight to Zambia that evening. Taking a chance, I walked into a side office where a manager with the most severe look on her face peered at me from across her desk. I thought I wasn't going to get anywhere with her but I recognised her brightly coloured dress as a style from the Shangaan culture. 'Tamanini, Mum,' I respectfully greeted her and within fifteen minutes I exited her office with my temporary passport. Nowhere else in the world do you receive such compassionate service as from a civil servant in South Africa if you take the time to be respectful and speak to them in their own language. Even if it's just a greeting. I am always astounded by the goodwill I receive when I speak to complete strangers in their own language.

Once we got back to Londolozi after that first trip to London, it was clear our guests enjoyed being with two guides who enjoyed each other's company and who loved their work. And, more importantly, who were really good at what they did. London had sparked something in my relationship with Renias and as a team we started to benefit. We received generous US-dollar tips from international guests and were even taken on a few holidays at various locations around the world. I managed to purchase a flat in Sandton in Johannesburg and Renias built a house so big some people call it the 'Nkandla' of Dixie!

One evening when I told a group of bankers sitting in the Londolozi boma that Renias and my relationship had resulted in tangible benefits for not only the two of us but for the company, too, one of them asked if I knew of any actual financial benefits. 'Supported by what metric do you make that statement, Alex?' asked a sceptical banker. I didn't have an answer for him but I firmly believed our partnership had brought in great rewards for Londolozi. The simple fact was that we'd successfully tracked and found so many leopards for our guests and brought them enjoyment, and that was good enough for me. I wondered if that was a suitable metric, though. I left the boma that night feeling a little despondent after not being able to answer the banker's question with specifics.

Years later a guide casually asked me how much money I thought Tobe and Jack Wilson, a New York couple Renias and I have taken on safaris for 24 years, have spent at Londolozi. The couple only visit Londolozi if both Renias and I are available and if one of us isn't, they postpone their trip. Tobe and Jack know the individual leopards at Londolozi just as well as any guide working there. They have meticulously recorded every single leopard sighting we've had together in the last two decades. Having spent literally thousands of hours in a Land Rover watching animals together, Tobe and Jack have become dear friends and we love our regular visits to their beautiful home in upstate New York.

I did a rough calculation that they had spent at least R6 million at Londolozi over the last two decades and I figured this was a decent metric to gauge the value of positive and productive relationships within an organisation! I wish I'd known that figure the night the smirking young banker had questioned me. I would have shut him up very quickly!

One of the less obvious benefits of Renias's inaugural visit to London was that he got to see where many of our guests came from and how they lived. He personally witnessed the stresses and strains of busy city life and in some ways he had unintentionally conducted valuable market research. This gave him immense insight and confidence when dealing with foreign guests on our return. Years spent with wealthy guests at Londolozi had given Renias the impression that their lives were perfect; a notion Renias said many black people in South Africa have of their white counterparts. After visiting London he learnt that this was not necessarily true. Obviously people everywhere, including London, face their own challenges, and in some ways those issues mirror those found in Dixie. One universal issue is how children just like Renias's son, Nature, rarely see their parents due to economic circumstances forcing them to leave their homes to find work to be able to provide for their families. This can be seen as similar to busy Londoners who leave home early in the morning and return late from work, sometimes without seeing their children.

On a safari a few months after our return, an English guest asked how our trip had been; a question loaded with expectation of an answer indicating how amazing London had been. It's true that we had thoroughly enjoyed our time there and told the guest as much, but Renias leaned over a few minutes later and whispered to me, 'I prefer to be poor in Dixie than rich in London.'

London had deepened our relationship. Being in an unfamiliar place and having a common experience gave new meaning to our partnership. My visit to Dixie and our trip to London were personal investments we made in each other. Instead of only words – narrative that can be interpreted in a many ways – we had demonstrated to each other acts of intentional brotherhood. I subsequently learnt that the effort I'd made in taking Renias to London was far more important to him than any of the activities we engaged in while we were there. It is clear to me that the endeavour holds far greater gravitas than the content when building a relationship across a language and cultural divide. In other words, building unlikely relationships requires a healthy dose of the symbolic, the non-literal and the suggestive as a means to convey messages of intent.

I have found that people derive meaning from personal interactions and events that are symbolic in nature and they often carry more weight than what is objectively true. In many ways, I developed a sense of self that was largely missing through the social interactions and symbolic events that I shared with Renias. Both Renias and I, through our respective cultural lenses, had ascribed particular meaning to our trips to Dixie and London and that enhanced our relationship, especially at work.

The gift of Aloe

After a good few years working together, travelling together and experiencing life together, Renias and I found our stride and our relationship grew stronger. This was evident in the safari experiences we gave the guests and, during this time, tracking leopards was all I could think about. The prospect of testing my tracking skills against such an elusive animal, the immense technical challenge and, of course, the reward of finding the leopard, was almost overwhelming. I had learnt that 'tracking' a leopard didn't mean driving around the reserve and getting lucky by spotting one lying in a tree. Nor was it about responding to another guide's radio report of one found in a particular place on the reserve.

Witnessing the guests' delight at seeing a leopard in the wild motivated Renias and me, and after every game drive we compared notes with the other guides and trackers to get a full picture of all the animal activity. At supper in the boma every night, we regaled our guests with stories about tracking leopards and when I went to bed I would dream about where we would find fresh tracks the following morning. My life was consumed by leopards!

Strangely, there were no other guides as interested in the craft of tracking as I was and I had little to offer in the field of wildlife photography, which many of them were particularly keen on. When Boyd finished his psychology studies in Cape Town, he lived with me for a month during the time I was the environmental manager at Londolozi. In Boyd I found a kindred spirit who was as interested in the traditional skills of tracking as I was. He is the younger brother I never had and someone I've walked a long road with. Initially we shared a youthful mischievousness but over the years we developed a common quest for greater spiritual understanding. Boyd is a tracker of the human condition; he has an uncanny ability to quickly and clearly see someone's life trail with just a smattering of evidence. Most Saturday mornings Boyd and I practised our tracking skills together. It was our 'golf'; our time to express ourselves freely in the complex task of wildlife tracking without the expectations of guests or students. It was just us.

We've spent hundreds of hours of tracking animals and discussing how the art has influenced our lives and how it could help others too. One morning Boyd arrived at my house to collect me, and said, 'Alex, to be a technically better tracker one must adopt the mentality of a tracker', a comment that profoundly changed how I viewed the ancient skill. Successful leopard tracking is like winning a limited-overs cricket match – you need the requisite skill but luck is also a contributing factor. At the Tracker Academy, our top tracker students seldom achieve better than a 15 per cent success rate when they track leopards unassisted. The first problem is to follow the trail successfully, which can often be an exceedingly challenging task in itself. The second issue is to spot the leopard in the landscape once it's found; an entirely different matter.

Renias and I have often been in situations where we knew the animal was right there but we just could not see it. Leopards are masters of camouflage and if they decide to hide, it's unlikely you will see them. While out tracking one day we knew the leopard we were following was close as we had tracked it to a prominent termite mound, where we'd seen very fresh tracks and heard the birds alarming. Scanning the shaded areas of the surrounding bush, I heard a soft blowing sound, almost like a gentle puffing, and then a brief flash of white. The under part of the leopard's tail was twitching in the thicket to my left and the animal was lying crouched under a bush no more than 3 metres away. It stared up at me intensely and hissed when our eyes met.

Renias and I were fiercely competitive with the other guides and trackers and we often counted the number of leopards we had found by consulting the sightings book in the ranger's room to establish our strike rate. One particular tracker, by the name of Richard Siwela, consistently beat us. He'd started as a tracker at Londolozi in 1972, some twelve years before Renias. Richard tracked leopards every day for twenty years before most other game lodges even cottoned on to the fact that using trackers was helpful in finding animals. He was a surly and cynical man, who was always immaculately turned out, and between game drives he would sit on his favourite tree stump outside his house, polishing his boots. Despite his advanced age, Richard didn't have a single grey hair and Renias told me that Richard polished his head with black shoe polish to keep his hair black – that's how important it was for him to maintain a dapper appearance!

Richard wasn't partial to pleasantries and, at times, displayed contempt for young guides. With the exception of Stompie Marais, a bright and confident young man not intimidated by Richard, people were afraid to work with him as one of his tactics was to correct the guide he was working with, in front of guests, if he thought they were expounding myths about an animal. He often humiliated the guides by calling them 'mamparas' if they did something he deemed silly in the bush.

He once said to me, 'Majombane, you and Renias are lazy. Why you come home if you haven't found the leopard?' As far as Richard was concerned, if he was finding leopards, he was doing his job just fine. As James Hendry said, 'Richard could spot a fake a hundred miles away,' and he had little time for new guides who pretended to know what they were doing.

He loved to track leopards as much as we did, but he found watching animals on game drives a waste of time and a hindrance to his job as a leopard tracker. By Renias's own admission, Richard remains the best leopard tracker at Londolozi, with a success rate that must have been consistently in the high 70 per cent range. Richard tracked leopards consistently for more than four decades and eventually retired from Londolozi in 2018. I think that Richard has successfully tracked and found more leopards than any tracker in South Africa, perhaps even in Africa. I doubt even the ancient hunter-gatherers would have had reason to track leopards on the consistent and focused basis Richard did.

On most days, Richard went out alone to track leopards. He'd leave camp at 11am once all the trackers were back from their morning game drives and then meticulously and painstakingly follow the trail of a leopard until he found it. He would succeed despite all the other trackers' failed attempts that morning. Notwithstanding the fact that a fleet of Land Rovers, as well as the guides and trackers had invariably driven and walked over the faint trail of tracks.

That persistent, tactical and skilful tracking gave wings to what is now a highly successful ecotourism industry in the Sabi Sands Game Reserve. Richard wasn't just a tracker; he was a founding member of an entire industry. Londolozi and the surrounding private game reserves have the original trackers to thank for the unmatched leopard viewing in that area.

Richard's tracking was a perfect example of how his personality shaped his tracking skills. He was systematic in his approach and the combination of his ability to discern even the faintest track on the ground and an uncanny capacity to predict the leopards' movements put Richard in a league of his own. And I loved that he knew it. He referred to himself as 'Siwela Number One' and if you look carefully at any photograph taken of Richard at Londolozi, you will notice him casually holding up his index finger to remind us of his status as the premier tracker. If there was ever a 'leopard man' in Africa, it is Richard Siwela.

Tracking could sometimes take hours and our longest trailing mission lasted almost ten hours while trying to locate an old male leopard. Because leopards tread very lightly on the ground and their spoor are a mere 8 centimetres in length, their tracks can easily be overlooked. The tracks often appear as smudges on hard ground and people are usually incredulous when shown a track, such is the faint nature of their impressions; a natural characteristic of leopards, right down to their footprint.

I've watched novice trackers stomp over a trail, even in loose sand where the tracks are reasonably clear. And if the tracks are over hard ground they become near impossible to see, let alone interpret, especially for a tracker sitting on the front of a Land Rover travelling at 40 kilometres an hour. A track that crosses the road, as opposed to one following the path of the road, can be easily missed by a tracker sitting on the seat on the bonnet of the vehicle. It isn't possible to follow a leopard's trail track for track like you would a dog on the beach and it represents the most complex form of tracking. You seldom see clear and conspicuous evidence, and partial and obscured tracks are usually the typical signs when tracking a leopard.

Renias and my strategy to find a leopard is for him to concentrate on seeing a track impression on the road while I look out for things such as kill remains, vulture activity, and many other signs. In the early days, we'd often receive news of fresh tracks found by another tracker or guide and that sometimes had an impact on our plans; either to keep following our tracks or to leave them and 'leapfrog' ahead to where the fresher ones had been found. Over time, we found those reports became less reliable and because tracking a leopard takes a while, the distraction caused by false reports made us lose too much valuable time. This meant we were forced to go to areas with little or no game-drive activity to find and follow tracks on our own.

Renias developed a technique a few years into our tracking together, where he tuned into the impressions he saw on the ground that were the general size and shape of a leopard's track but more importantly had a uniquely darkened colour that signified a fresh impression. Like a computer program, he developed a mental search image that became his frame of reference for finding faint and obscure leopard tracks. As the years rolled by and as his experience grew, I witnessed that search image become more refined and more accurate.

He would tell me to stop the Land Rover and we would get out and walk several metres down the road trying to establish whether what he had seen was a track and how old it was; no easy task on hard stony ground. Renias often spotted tracks that other trackers had driven past and this really irritated him. It was also one of the reasons that prompted him to suggest we start our own tracking school. Ten years later we were fortunate to co-create an academy to train young people as professional trackers, but it would still be a decade before that became a reality.

Tracking leopards requires a creative approach that usually compels you to make use of deductive reasoning to create a mental picture of the animal's activities. This is a process of inquiry whereby you test theories of animal movement by determining whether the outcome is consistent with the evidence observed by the tracker. As a simple example, if the leopard's tracks are headed in the direction of a cool shady riverbed at midday, it is reasonable to deduce that the animal may be resting in the donga having just fed. This approach only works for those trackers who possess both exceptional technical competence as well as refined understanding of animal behaviour and local knowledge. Competent trackers have a good retentive memory, technical knowledge of track evidence and are both detail-oriented as well as creative.

One afternoon, Renias and I lost the tracks of a leopard we were following in difficult terrain, but instead of giving up, Renias suggested we check a grove of marula trees on the sandy crest that was up ahead. The intense heat that day made the tall, shady marula trees the perfect spot for leopards seeking shade and Renias had also noticed fresh evidence of an impala herd heading in the same direction. A few minutes later, we found the leopard stalking the impala and after an unsuccessful chase, it climbed one of the marula trees to rest in the relatively cool breeze that was blowing. From an outsider's perspective it must've looked like magic that Renias found the leopard that afternoon but by merging the evidence he observed, combined with his local knowledge, he identified a pattern of the leopard's movement and behaviour.

The best trackers are those who are able to find solutions by making connections between seemingly unrelated pieces of evidence. In this case, the presence of the marula trees and the impala tracks heading up the slope of the hill were two isolated, yet vital, pieces of the puzzle that Renias picked up. Depending on a tracker's individual personality, tracking problems are solved either systematically, by creating hypotheses, or by intuition.

Renias uses a blend of systematic and abstract (also called

'speculative tracking') approaches in his tracking style while Richard preferred to stay on the trail, a preference borne of his unique ability to recognise faint tracks even in exceedingly difficult substrate. As time passed, Renias used his intuition more and more and the words, 'I have a feeling it's gone this way', is a Renias utterance I've heard hundreds of times while tracking with him.

Unfortunately, because it's challenging to explain what intuition or unconscious reasoning is, it has a poor reputation in the field of science. Renias and other expert trackers with years of tracking animals over and over again have developed an abundance of unconscious mental links that, when triggered by a piece of familiar evidence, such as a track or alarm call, provides them with a mental picture or the larger composition of what the animal is doing.

Caroline Myss, *New York Times* bestselling author of many books, including *Anatomy of the Spirit* and *Invisible Acts of Power*, was a guest at Londolozi who Renias and I took on safari some years ago. Caroline is a medical intuitive and from a very young age she has been able to intuitively detect health problems, with astonishing accuracy, in people she has never met. She recounted how as a young girl she was able to detect illness in a friend of her mother's after meeting her for the first time. Caroline doesn't know how she knew but it turned out the woman had a terminal illness.

Our time in the bush with Caroline was fascinating and her take on intuition is that we are not limited to five senses and that we have numerous sensing skills, including emotional and intuitive. She says, 'Intuition is an inherent sense that develops in you just as you develop eyes, ears and your other senses.' The challenge today is to understand how your intuitive nature communicates with you as it is the most active and authentic part of who you are. It's your inner self that has become highly attuned to everything and everyone around you and it is a form of intelligence that we all need to learn to trust.

Having taught educated and affluent people, as well low-income and often illiterate people, I've noticed that those constrained by the intensely cerebral approach to life, often associated with Western education, are less trusting of that 'gut' feeling. In contrast, men such as Renias, Richard, Pokkie, master tracker and one of the head trackers at Tracker Academy, and Eric, my early mentor who passed away tragically at Ngala, seemed more inclined to trust 'that' feeling and therefore had a greater chance of developing their trailing skills to a point where they transcended their reliance on only the evidence.

Having said all that, though, tracking is a practical skill that anyone can learn. It is not an unexplained mystical skill reserved for a few privileged master hunter-gatherers or shaman. Like any skill or vocation, you either have an aptitude for it or not, but with effortful practice you can become a competent tracker. Renias and I have seen this with our tracker students; young men who have never been to a wilderness area or seen a wild animal, let alone their tracks, cultivate remarkable tracking skills in just one year of intensive training.

Many of them graduate with the ability to track and find a lion, unassisted, in challenging terrain over a period of hours. Building our tracking skills and understanding behaviour was important to Renias and me as we believed that the better trackers we became, the greater our chances were of engendering trust with certain individual leopards. This was something that Renias knew from experience was only possible if we were interacting with the leopards on foot regularly and sensitively.

Renias and I started forming a relationship with a leopard called Mhangene a few years into our tracking. The Shangaan word 'mhangene' means 'aloe' as her initial territory was located in an area with an abundance of aloes. Mhangene was first encountered in 1991 and from the outset she had a very relaxed temperament. Unlike most of the leopards in the reserve, we didn't know her ancestry, but she frequented the Mhangene donga and eventually established a territory further east along the dry Mxabene riverbed.

That dry riverbed forms the core area of leopard viewing at Londolozi and, as Mhangene was a small animal, we were surprised that she could hold such prime territory. The area is made up of dense riparian thicket, tall evergreen trees, ancient floodplain pans and an abundance of grey duiker, nyala and bushbuck, making it perfect leopard habitat.

When one of Mhangene's female cubs matured, she relocated her territory westwards to allow space for her daughter; a common practice whereby mother leopards shift their territory to accommodate a daughter. We called that daughter the Mxabene female because her core territory was centred around the Mxabene riverbed and its associated dongas. Young male leopards, by contrast, invariably become nomadic and move greater distances from their natal territory.

Mhangene produced a number of litters over the years but sadly lost most of her cubs to raids by lion and hyaena. Her inexperience in selecting appropriately safe den sites and her reluctance to hoist her kills into trees meant she had a poor record of raising cubs.

The Mxabene female was Mhangene's first real success at raising a daughter and I remember watching her as an eleven-month-old subadult, recently independent of her mother, trying to make her first kill. She spent ten unsuccessful days in the same tree, hunting the same squirrel and playing a game of test-match-like cat and mouse. Something I'm sure the squirrel enjoyed when it finally realised how incompetent the young leopard was that it was dealing with! But a few weeks later in the pelting rain, we watched Mxabene take down and kill a fully grown adult male impala like a seasoned hunter. The precociousness of such a young leopard killing such a big animal astounded me, but unfortunately her inexperience again came to the fore when she had her entire meal stolen by a nomadic male lion. The intensive alarm calling from the impala herd brought in the adult lion and I don't think Mxabene even managed a single bite of her kill.

Mhangene remained our favourite leopard to track and for some reason we had a very good record of tracking and finding her. On one occasion we followed her tracks into a vast open area with long grass. It was midday on a particularly hot summer's day and the clayey black cotton soil, endemic to the area and terrain, made our progress slow. We stopped to watch a vulture fly over in the hope it would lead us to her, but then we heard a group of banded mongooses making an alarm call that we decided to investigate. We found Mhangene stalking the mongooses out in the open near an old quarry. The breeze was in our favour so she wasn't aware of our presence but the fact that she was hunting mongooses at midday meant she was probably desperately hungry. As we approached, one of the mongooses saw us and sounded another alarm, alerting Mhangene to our presence. She casually looked back at us, stood up and wandered off. The hunt was over and the mongooses were left to their own devices.

It was lunchtime by that point and all the game drives had returned to camp so I turned around to go fetch the Land Rover when Renias said to me, 'Leave the Landy, mfo, let's walk with her.' We knew Mhangene was a calm animal but it seemed absurd to try to view a wild leopard on foot in this way. Under normal circumstances, finding and meeting a leopard on foot solicits either an angry response from the animal or they hide or bound away in fear. A guest standing up in an open Land Rover can cause a reaction, that's how sensitive leopards, and indeed all animals, are to the human form and all that it represents, when on foot. But that day I sensed Renias wanted to experiment, so we slowly and quietly started walking with her as she meandered through the grass. Initially we maintained a distance of about 80 metres and every so often I noticed her ears pointing backwards as she listened to us but didn't even give us a glance.

Mhangene then headed towards a russet bushwillow woodland on the edge of a clearing, beyond which is a small waterhole. She paused intermittently to look and listen, eagerly trying to detect prey. She then investigated a termite-mound entrance dug by an aardvark and climbed on top of it, using the elevation to her advantage. She spent several moments on the mound scanning in all directions and there was no doubt that she was on the prowl. By this stage we'd closed the gap between us to about 40 metres and there was still no reaction from her. Every so often she stopped to sniff the ground and then turned around, scraped the ground with her hind legs and sprayed urine backwards onto a bush and then carried on. We knew she was near the edge of her territory and wondered whether the sniffing had something to do with a rival female or a potential mate. Renias and I smelt the scent markings and they had an odour similar to that of burnt popcorn. Some markings smelt more intense than others but we weren't sure of the reason why.

At one point, two starlings screeched in alarm and I could see that irritated Mhangene because she glared scornfully at them and when one flew close by, she flashed a snarl at it but made no sound. She lifted her tail exposing the white underside almost in an attempt to placate the squawking birds as if to say, 'You foolish bird, I'm not hunting you so keep quiet.' Fortunately, the tail move worked and the birds flew off and left her to hunt in peace. The element of surprise is vital for a hunting predator and animals of different species will heed each other's alarm calls and Mhangene knew this, hence her agitation with the starlings. I considered for a while the host of challenges this poor animal had to endure to find food.

Once the starlings flew off, she proceeded slowly again, stopping briefly to observe a bateleur eagle descending in the distance – a possible indicator of a carcass or a rival predator. Being relatively small and solitary predators, leopards will always try to avoid confrontation with other large carnivores for fear of being injured and rendered incapable of feeding themselves. Unlike lions and hyaenas, which have their prides and clans to sustain them, a wounded leopard risks starvation.

A lilac-breasted roller then started to alarm but from a more northerly direction and I watched Mhangene observe it momentarily and then carry on. Like a tracker, she was identifying and, I assume, interpreting all the evidence around her as it became available. To what extent does she have the capacity to create a mental picture of the activity around her like a tracker does, I wondered. I considered how much she was sensing that we couldn't and I pondered what was going through her mind, if anything at all. It occurred to me then that this leopard represented the ultimate exponent of awareness and alertness. She derived her awareness from being completely in the moment in a calm and mindful process of noticing. Mhangene was aware and alert and alive to everything going on around her and she took nothing for granted. I thought about her wordless world and how it probably benefitted her as a 'tracker'. She was free of the constant stories of the mind, the ceaseless narrative that causes distraction in humans, and was fully present and utterly focused on the task at hand.

As she entered the thicket, she froze and became fixated on something up ahead. 'She's seen something,' whispered Renias. The dense vegetation meant our visibility was much more limited so to stay with her we needed to get closer and I started to wonder how much more we could push our experiment. By now, we were no more than 20 metres away from her. For the first time she looked at us and with a look I took to mean, 'Don't make a noise,' she crouched down. Renias and I did the same and we all scanned the bush ahead, an unlikely team of hunters. For a few brief moments we were all members of the same hunting band, a curious human-animal coalition. I couldn't help smiling with the joy I was experiencing in that moment. This was a level of immersion into nature I didn't think was possible, something I had been hoping to achieve since that fateful day with the Tugwaan female.

Renias and I still couldn't see anything but we were being guided by the leopard. She dropped into a full stalk and I was astonished at how low she got to the ground. The flies, the biting ants and the sweat on my face were all distractions that I had to find a way to ignore, especially as we didn't want to spoil the hunt for her. Then about 50 metres ahead of us, a grey duiker appeared in a small opening in the bush, browsing peacefully. The wind was in our favour and the small antelope was unaware of our presence and I wondered whether Mhangene had deliberately considered the wind direction. Having watched countless lions and leopards hunt, they don't necessarily take the wind direction into account but Mhangene remained totally focused on the duiker. Every time the duiker moved, she moved. If it looked up, she froze and got closer to the ground. The tip of her tail twitched restlessly, perhaps evidence of her exuberance but her gaze never left the duiker. I signalled to Renias that we shouldn't go any further for fear of alerting the duiker. He too was smiling at the incredible experience we were having. Our awkward stalking gait was becoming far too cumbersome and noisy so we waited for the duiker to move and then backed off slowly, bit by bit. A few moments later we heard Mhangene rush forward but she missed and unfortunately the duiker got away.

About a year later we started noticing Mhangene making an unusual chuffing sound whenever she walked past our Land Rover. She would make short intermittent puffing sounds by blowing air through her nostrils. I'd never heard a leopard do that before and it didn't seem threatening in any way, nor did she seem stressed or agitated. We'd find her walking in the bush and once she saw us, she would turn and walk towards our vehicle making chuffing sounds, almost as if she was greeting us. It was that obvious.

One of the guides used to joke and say that Mhangene was in love with Renias and me! This happened sporadically but it was very noticeable. I asked the other guides whether any of them had seen this behaviour before and only one of them had. I later discovered that this form of communication among cats is called 'prusten', which translates to 'chuffing'. 'Prusten' is the German word for sneeze or snort and the behaviour has been recorded only in tigers and snow and clouded leopards. Chuffing is by all accounts a non-threatening vocalisation used by cats to greet each other and during courtship. John Varty, of the famous tiger project in the Karoo, told me that his tigers chuffed when they greeted him so it seems it could also be a form of recognition.

We were dumbfounded. Did Mhangene recognise us in some way? Was she purposely greeting us? Renias was convinced that she knew us and that the puffing was a simple greeting. Considering that domestic cats recognise their owners, I don't see any reason why Mhangene couldn't recognise us. Had this leopard seen us so many times over the past years that she could distinguish us from the other guides and trackers? Renias believes our time hunting with Mhangene was a turning point in our relationship with her, allowing a kinship to grow. On some level, perhaps she viewed us merely as benevolent human companions, non-competing predators that represented no threat to her. Whatever the reason, Renias and I felt we had a deep connection with Mhangene and the more we tracked her, the more accustomed she became to us being close to her on foot.

Because of the highly elusive nature of leopards, viewing them always happens on their terms and if they become agitated for any reason, they simply slip out of sight. I've witnessed many leopards glare in irritation at the occupants of game vehicles until eventually they become so annoyed that they disappear. What made Mhangene's behaviour interesting is that leopards are an independent, solitary species and usually don't 'do' groups when they are adults – even a 'group' made up of just Renias and me.

Jon Varty told me that the leopard cubs he'd raised over the years started out almost completely habituated but, as they got older, they became increasingly more distant compared to the lions, tigers and cheetahs he'd also raised from newborn. It is for this reason efforts to re-wild captive-bred leopards have been far more successful than those attempted with many of the other large cats.

The power of Renias and my relationship with Mhangene allowed us to immerse ourselves into the life of a wild leopard. At a time when humanity's connection with the natural world is under such duress, interactions and bonds like the one we had with Mhangene are symbolic of what is possible.

Mhangene got spat in the eye by a Mozambique spitting cobra a few years later. Although it didn't seem to directly affect her ability to hunt, she was old by then and physically far less agile so it is likely that it did contribute to her reduced proficiency. A few months after this, we stopped seeing Mhangene's tracks. We never found her body and we don't know how she died. She was simply gone.

My grandparents, Nana and Beepa, with Missy and me.
ALEX PERSONAL COLLECTION

Missy and me at Trefoil.
ALEX PERSONAL COLLECTION

Our family together again, and my parents divorced and reunited after twenty years.
ALEX PERSONAL COLLECTION

In the bathtub at Dixie Village.
JAMES MARSHALL

In London in 1999.
ALEX AND RENIAS PERSONAL COLLECTION

Tracking leopards.
GRANT ASHFIELD

Renias in the Ferrari in London.
ALEX AND RENIAS PERSONAL COLLECTION

Early days as motivational speakers.
ALEX AND RENIAS PERSONAL COLLECTION

The best leopard viewing in the world.
DAVID DAMPIER

Renias and me as young
guides at Londolozi.
ALEX AND RENIAS PERSONAL COLLECTION

Renias's brothers, Elmon and Phineas, and their father, Judas.
IAN THOMAS

Renias and his mother, Anania.
JAMES MARSHALL

Fund-raising trip to New York in 2013.
ALEX AND RENIAS PERSONAL COLLECTION

Tracker Academy students in 2018.
JOE GROSEL

With Tracker Academy graduate, Trevor Makukule, in 2018.
GRANT ASHFIELD

Captivated by a giant anteater while tracking in Pantanal, Brazil.
ALEX AND RENIAS PERSONAL COLLECTION

A contemplative moment while tracking.
JAMES TYRRELL

Tracking black bears in California.
ALEX AND RENIAS PERSONAL COLLECTION

Our beloved Mhangene Female.
WARREN PEARSON

Renias gives an enthralling speech at my wedding in 2014.
ALEX AND RENIAS PERSONAL COLLECTION

The jaguar viewing at Caiman has improved exponentially since starting the tracking and habituation project.
MARIO HABERFELD

Tracking pumas in Patagonia, Chile.
ALEX AND RENIAS PERSONAL COLLECTION

Viewing pumas in Patagonia.
ALEX AND RENIAS PERSONAL COLLECTION

Filming of wildlife tracking simulation.
GRANT ASHFIELD

A poacher at heart

The current rhino-poaching crisis may have started in 2008 in South Africa, but prior to that small commercial poachers were active in the park, although nowhere near the levels we see today. The greater Kruger National Park anti-poaching units dealt mostly with subsistence hunters, local people killing animals, albeit illegally, for food for themselves and their families. They usually target small animals because their use of weaponry, such as wire snares, is often antiquated. Syndicate poachers are the ones making headlines and they make use of advanced weapons, including helicopters and night-vision technology, as they target high-value animal species such as rhino, elephant, lion and pangolin. Commercial poachers are well organised and kill for profit; they are often the same organisations that run the local drug cartels – in other words, they are professional and well-resourced criminals. It is the commercial hunters who have the greatest impact on endangered species such as elephant and rhino in Africa.

Prior to colonisation, African people utilised the land for

survival. As we discovered in Renias's early beginnings, local Shangaan people moved periodically, resulting in somewhat sustainable utilisation of natural resources in a given area. That said, there is also ample and clear historical evidence of reverence shown for wild animals by hunter-gatherers as well as spiritual customs that prohibited killing of certain species. But with colonisation the trade in animal parts intensified, increasing the value of wild animals and creating wealth for some local people, while at the same time politicising the hunting.

In the early 2000s, when I was the environmental manager at Londolozi, we started to experience an increase in subsistence poaching incidents in the northern extent of the reserve, a remote area with little human infrastructure. A poacher or a group of poachers was setting long lines of wire snares to capture animals such as impala, warthog and even wildebeest. Ecologically, the reserve could deal with the loss of a few antelope but when a beautiful black-maned male lion was killed, we realised we were dealing with a commercial poacher. Few people eat lion meat but their bones, claws and teeth are valuable in the medicine markets of Asia. The problem is that lions are far easier to catch than most other animals so you only need to use bait to poison them or snare the animal. For a game reserve that relies on photographic safaris for income, losing a physically impressive territorial lion is a disaster for the tourism operation. A resident lion can be viewed by guests thousands of times in its lifetime and is therefore a tremendously valuable asset provided it stays alive.

A POACHER AT HEART

I was told by the head of the anti-poaching unit at the time that the poaching incidents were the work of one man. To protect his identity, I'll call him Jon. Jon was operating as if the northern part of the reserve was his personal hunting ground. At one point, he allegedly poisoned a flock of vultures and sold their heads to a traditional healer for about R600 for each bird.

The Shangaan elders told me about the local belief that vultures can predict the future and that white-backed vultures dream of death when they sleep and are then able to find a carcass early the next morning before the sun rises. This belief is in direct contradiction to the notion that African vultures find their food using their sense of sight from high in the sky. The belief that vultures can predict the future has been created because occasionally they are seen feeding on a carcass at first light, before the Earth has warmed and before the thermal air currents that usually carry them have developed.

The Old World African species of vulture predominantly make use of their eyesight to locate carcasses in the open savanna but they have also been observed using their sense of smell to find meat on cold overcast days. However, this is uncommon behaviour and differs from what most people believe to be the means by which vultures locate their food. Sadly, there are only about 2 000 pairs of white-backed vultures left in the greater Kruger National Park. Research suggests that vultures have declined by 67 per cent in southern Africa in the last 30 years.

Over a ten-year period, many anti-poaching units in the southern Kruger Park tried to apprehend Jon but none of them was successful in capturing him. There were stories that he had special powers that prevented him from being caught and he apparently slept covered in animal fat so that if anyone tried to grab him in the night, he could slip away out of their grasp. The lard was said to be specially prepared with medicinal herbs so as to give Jon extra power to escape. Some of the local people told me Jon could run like the wind and that's why no one could catch him. Rumour had it that you could 'order' an impala from Jon at 3 o'clock in the afternoon and he would deliver it to you that evening, like a Mr Delivery in the bush. Jon was a commercial poacher, very good at staying at large, and his business was seemingly doing very well.

Jon was clearly an experienced bush man and seldom left clear tracks to follow. Whenever the anti-poaching team conducted patrols and night watches, Jon somehow found out about it and we then wouldn't see evidence of his presence for a few weeks thereafter. Eventually, after months of evasion, I asked Renias and his brother Elmon to assist us in finding Jon. I asked them to try to find out his real identity as well as where he lived, and I promised Renias I would not have him arrested. I just wanted to talk to him.

A few days later, Renias returned with information that the poacher went by the name of Jon and that he lived in a village called Utah, north of Dixie. The next day Renias and I travelled up to Utah to find Jon. We found his house and stood in his yard amongst his home-made gym equipment crafted from various vehicle spare parts. A battered old car also stood in his plot and when I asked Jon if it worked, he said that it did but the only problem was, 'I use the trees for braking,' he said, laughing loudly. Wearing only a pair of grey shorts, Jon was in exceptional condition. He was clearly a man who lived an intensely physical lifestyle and he was all muscle and veins. I was surprised how comfortable Jon seemed around us after a relatively short space of time.

Our conversation with Jon followed and I said to him, 'Jon, we know you have been poaching and we know about the male lion and vultures you killed.' I reminded him that his luck evading the anti-poaching police would someday run out and I put it to him that his life would be far less stressful if he wasn't having to constantly look over his shoulder for fear of being caught and thrown in jail.

He nodded knowingly and I went on to explain that tracking animals for tourists to view could be just as lucrative as selling bushmeat to the locals. It was clear that he got the message and so I asked him to tell me what his dreams were for the future. I suppose this was a strange question to ask a hardened poacher but he replied in earnest and said, 'Learn English.' He wanted to learn to read and write English properly. 'That's why I do this job,' said Jon referring to his lack of literacy as the reason for his 'unemployed' status. The fact that he used the word 'job' made me realise that Jon viewed poaching no differently to any other regular nine-to-five occupation.

By all accounts, he was a talented tracker and was simply using his skills to earn a living. I couldn't imagine the urgency that comes with developing a skill in response to a primal need simply to eat and survive. We offered for Jon to come to Londolozi for a few months and I told him we would trade him a place to stay, food to eat and the use of our local school in return for a favour. We had been reliably informed that there was another poacher operating in the same area in the reserve and I wanted Jon to help us catch that poacher. I was also interested in formally testing Jon's tracking skills to establish how he stacked up against the regular tourism trackers at Londolozi. In addition, Boyd wanted to immerse himself in the life of a poacher and learn the art of tracking from a different perspective. Jon agreed to come with us. Dave Varty recognised that if we could establish a productive relationship with Jon, his skills could be invaluable to a private game reserve and he supported my decision to enlist Jon's help.

Boyd and I returned and collected Jon, along with his wire snares and metal spear that he folded into a small black sports bag with a few of his possessions. We had to smuggle him through the reserve gate into Londolozi as the local anti-poaching unit in the area had by now got wise to our plan. We pitched a tent for Jon in the middle of the staff village right outside Renias's house so that we could keep an eye on him, and I was surprised at how many of the staff actually knew him. Jon fitted in straight away with the rest of the staff and I wondered how many of them knew he was a poacher. A staff member jokingly asked me why I'd brought 'Mr Checkers' to Londolozi, so I suppose that answered my question as to whether people knew him!

On one of our first trips to the bush with Jon, Boyd and I asked him to follow the track of a young male leopard so we could gauge his trailing skills. While following the leopard's trail, Jon noticed a fresh track of a hyaena running in a perpendicular direction. 'We follow this one, it is better,' exclaimed Jon. I looked at Boyd and we shrugged our shoulders and decided to give Jon a chance to prove himself. Jon broke away from the leopard trail and started following the hyaena tracks instead. He started to run slowly, very subtly mimicking a hyaena's lope. Boyd and I followed him and were amused by his ridiculous hyaena-type gait. I was fascinated to see what Jon could do and in broken English he explained that he thought the hyaena knew where the leopard was. The tracks headed south towards the Mxabene donga and past a small watering hole and the longer Jon followed the hyaena trail, the faster he 'loped'. Initially, he followed track for track in a systematic fashion but he soon started to speculate, in an almost completely irreverent way, and was moving so fast that I doubted there was much planning and projecting going on in his mind. The pace he was moving at seemed unsafe as we could easily have run into a buffalo bull standing quietly in a thicket. This wasn't just fast tracking, this was a cavalier demonstration by someone intent on finding the animal as fast as possible. There was no regard for any formal safety protocols and he was not at all concerned with what we might have thought of his conduct. But I don't suppose that is really a primary concern for a poacher. There was an urgency in Jon that I hadn't seen in other trackers; an approach that was no doubt developed in response to constant efforts at evading the anti-poaching police as well as a desperate need of having to find meat as efficiently as possible. Unlike tourism trackers, Jon's approach appeared to lack any respect for animals and it didn't seem to worry him that we might have disturbed the leopard if we found it. He relied on his athleticism and momentum to catch up with his quarry, in the same way African wild dogs trot when on the hunt, as well as to keep himself safe.

Ten minutes later, Jon stopped us and gestured ahead, tapping his ear to indicate that he'd heard something. We stood still for a few moments but all I could hear was heavy breathing from having just run about 3 kilometres. Jon told us a leopard was calling, so we waited a few moments but still didn't hear anything. By now, I had become suspicious of Jon's ability and pondered whether he was just winging it. How can a tracker move at such a pace and still be able to see and hear evidence? Jon continued and a few minutes later he gestured to us again. I concentrated hard to try to hear something. I then just made out the tail end of a leopard's rasping call in the distance and while the call wasn't loud, we could hear that the animal was reasonably close by. Jon slowed and began to stalk like a predator, using the wind to his advantage. This was also unusual behaviour as we weren't accustomed to stalking leopards this way. Eventually we broke out of a small thicket and found a male leopard feeding on an impala carcass in a tree. Two hyaenas lay near the base of the tree, waiting patiently for their chance to rob the leopard of its meat. Jon's ability to anticipate the hyaena's movements, despite his unorthodox approach, had paid off and I was suitably impressed. It did occur to me that he might have got lucky that day but I liked his eccentric method of tracking and I looked forward to hearing what Boyd would learn from Jon.

That evening, Boyd and I sat around the fire with Jon and he told us story after story about his life as a poacher. I watched him carefully, with a certain degree of scepticism as he opened his second quart of Black Label with his fingers, as he recounted more events. Some of his stories seemed too far-fetched to believe and I doubted the truth of his tale about catching a blue wildebeest near the Lebombo mountains in the Kruger Park, butchering it and then carrying the animal 70 kilometres back to his house in Utah. A wildebeest's live weight can be anything from 260 kilograms so I was doubtful this was physically possible and I struggled to believe Jon. His outlandish stories started to make other people in the boma laugh, and the stories became more fanciful the more Black Label he consumed.

Whether or not the stories were true, the fact was that Jon had spent all of his adult life hunting illegally and this had afforded him a unique form of tracking proficiency. He had shown us what he was capable of and I liked that he was unconventional in his approach. I started to wonder whether he had it in him to change his ways, if he was given the opportunity. If so, he would be helping us in the process and would perhaps realise there were other lucrative, and more importantly, legal ways to make a living. In hindsight, it was naive of me to think Jon would abandon his previous life simply to satisfy what I'm sure he thought were the 'theoretical benefits' of formal employment.

Jon and Boyd began conducting informal anti-poaching patrols in the bush and it was clear from the outset that Jon understood the modus operandi of the other local poachers in the area. Within the first week, they caught a poacher who'd laid a string of nearly a hundred wire snares in dense woodland. The man they apprehended was known to Jon and I'm sure he must have felt a pang of guilt when the young man was hauled off to the Skukuza prison. As we had anticipated, the incidents of wire snares set up in the bush dropped dramatically while Jon was at Londolozi.

Aside from the anti-poaching patrols, Jon and Boyd started focusing on tracking lion and leopard for game drives. A wonderfully mutually beneficial relationship formed in terms of which Jon taught Boyd his ways of the wild and Boyd showed Jon how his skills could be effectively utilised in a formal ecotourism operation. We were pleased in our efforts to have effectively removed a very successful and notorious poacher from the southern Kruger National Park and we slowly integrated Jon into life at Londolozi as a tracker, a job he appeared to enjoy.

There is much talk of rehabilitating poachers to work in the conservation industry, almost as if poaching is merely a functional money-making imperative. There is a notion that poachers are waiting to be employed in a legal capacity of some sort and that they *want* to be employed. Jon had made a good living supplying fresh meat on a daily basis to the local villages in his capacity as a poacher, and not only was he reasonably financially independent, he had his freedom and wasn't constrained by the usual terms of formal employment. Education as a means of preventing crime and as a form of promoting a culture of lawfulness is all well and good if you've been afforded the opportunity to learn about nature in conservation lessons or if you've simply gone to a decent school, but Jon hadn't had any of those opportunities. He had been one of those children who stared jealously through high fortified wire fences watching the shiny 'mabenzies' and fat animals pass by in the reserve. Conservation education prepares children to associate the impact of their current actions with the future benefit of the ecology and wildlife but without any education Jon viewed wildlife merely as a form of currency that could be traded.

I don't think Jon ever considered a future without the fancy cars and wild animals roaming around the game reserve or how their disappearance would affect him financially. As far as he was concerned, in the microcosm of his life, the way it was set up, and his daily fight for survival, nature would provide abundantly in perpetuity, as it had for his ancestors. Jon thought that killing a few impalas, vultures and the odd lion wouldn't matter very much to the vast Kruger National Park, but what he didn't think about was the number of other small-scale poachers also active in the reserve, doing the same thing. He gave little consideration to the sustainability of his actions and what the future might look like in the face of the unmitigated slaughter of wild animals. If given the opportunity to learn, Jon would have been taught the mutual human-animal benefits of the wildlife economy.

Although Jon spent a significant amount of time in the Kruger National Park throughout his life, he had never formally visited the park to understand its greater mission to conserve wildlife. As a result, he saw the game reserve as one massive business opportunity that he exploited with little emotional connection. In the time that I spent with Jon, I gleaned that his job wasn't particularly pleasant but it was necessary for his survival and gave him the freedom that he needed.

One afternoon, I found Jon lifting weights, in his underpants, at the

Londolozi gym. The informality of the situation meant we struck up a casual conversation and I gently enquired what actually motivated him to hunt illegally. I wanted to understand on a deeper, perhaps emotional, level the reasons why someone would wilfully live the life of a poacher. 'I am dom,' he said to me, referring to his lack of education. 'What must I do?' he continued rhetorically, as he swung a dumb-bell above his head as unconventionally as he tracked leopards. His answer didn't really satisfy me as he could have looked for a job at a lodge as a tracker. There was something more to it that I needed to understand. While I could see that Jon believed he was unemployable in a classic sense, I knew he had intrinsic value to the ecotourism industry that he didn't realise he had.

Over the years, I have been amazed at how many talented trackers subconsciously believe their skills are valueless. This insecurity is possibly borne of a situation where conservation management has for generations subjected trackers to low-ranking jobs with menial remuneration and I felt a need to change this perception. I left the gym convinced that formal tracker and conservation ethics training was desperately needed to stem the flow of creating more 'Jons', and the conversation I'd been having with Renias to establish a school became that much more meaningful and urgent.

Renias, Elmon, Boyd and I all poured as much time, effort and intellectual property into our efforts with Jon as we possibly could. We genuinely wanted him to make a successful transition from an illegal hunter to a formally employed professional wildlife tracker, but it required him to internalise a fundamental shift in how he valued wildlife. Jon started joining the game drives to learn how to conduct a wildlife experience as a tourist tracker, and he spent time at the Londolozi learning centre learning to read, write and speak English. He successfully tracked animals in his eccentric way and it proved to be of great value to the tourist operation. Eventually, I found Jon a permanent tracker job at one of the neighbouring private game reserves because the low tracker turnover at Londolozi meant there were no vacancies. I didn't want to lose momentum with Jon and I desperately wanted him to see that living a life without crime could be sustainable and rewarding.

Jon quickly settled into his new formal ecotourism tracking job and I started receiving positive reports about him finding animals for the lodge guests, his unusual approach notwithstanding. The guide he was assigned to told me that Jon was like a 'wild horse bolting' when he started following tracks while the lodge manager gave me a less convincing report detailing that 'in his strange way' Jon was adding value to the guest experience at the lodge.

I occasionally phoned Jon to enquire how things were progressing in his job at the lodge but deep down I think I was 'fishing' to establish whether he'd successfully made the transition from a criminal to a legitimate tracker and, by all accounts, he had. Our calls were always upbeat and laced with the usual Jon-style storytelling, and as time passed I called Jon less often and instead got feedback on his performance via the bush telegraph.

Renias and I were thrilled at Jon's personal evolution, a lifestyle transformation that couldn't have been easy to make. Jon had truly abandoned his life as a poacher and was contributing to conservation efforts through ecotourism. He had formally entered the bourgeoning economy of wildlife and I heard he bought himself a new car – one that didn't need a tree to brake! Jon was earning a decent salary and, in addition, receiving generous tips from guests. A South African guest who had been on game drive with Jon told me how hard he had worked to find a pride of lions for the guests one morning, and his efforts prompted the group to pay for Jon's children to go to school.

In the meantime, the head of one of the anti-poaching units in the park, the man who had warned me not to bring Jon into the game reserve two years before, lost his job for alleged involvement in a rhino-poaching incident. What irony, I thought, and for the first time I realised how attractive and lucrative the rhino-poaching business was, irrespective of the colour of your skin, your background or your income level. Renias and I started including Jon's story in our motivational presentations as an example of how to think more creatively in dealing with conflict at work. A photograph of Jon was projected onto the screens of several JSE-listed companies and, in many ways, Jon became our star example of how the power of relationships can turn a negative into a positive. People loved Jon's success story because it was about personal triumph as well as a great example of the impact that productive relationships can have on business, humans and wildlife.

Ten years later, I received a call from the head guide at the lodge where Jon was working. He started the conversation by saying, 'It's your friend, Jon. He has been caught poaching red-handed.' Jon had been arrested during work hours by one of the Kruger Park section rangers for allegedly killing a rhino. He had been caught with a bloodied rhino horn in his bakkie on his way out of the reserve. Strangely, I found myself unshaken by the news, as if on some level I knew Jon would always be the same man, with the same fears, carrying the same get-rich-quick illusions he'd always possessed. I was told that Jon provided all the evidence and information to the police with little prompting; perhaps an indication that he knew his luck was finally up or that he thought it might help him avoid prosecution.

I often get asked when I recount Jon's story why I think he poached that rhino, and recounting the fable about the scorpion who begged the frog to carry him across the river is the only answer I have. The story goes that midway across the river the scorpion stung the frog and as they both started drowning, the frog asked, 'Why?' and the scorpion answered, 'I'm sorry. It's in my nature.' Jon threw away his life and is in jail, useful to no one. Everyone around him lost something when he became involved in poaching that rhino: Jon himself, his employer, the game reserve and the rhino. The conservation industry lost a rare talent and another young family was left vulnerable and having to fend for themselves without a provider and father.

Sometimes I think about what more we could have done to assist Jon. When you consider that about three-quarters of convicted criminals re-offend, and while Jon hadn't been convicted of anything when Renias and I first met him, the statistic shows an important pattern of behaviour that is spurred on by the poverty in our country. Jon was impulsive; he had little ability to delay his gratification and he did not have the foresight to grasp the consequences of his actions.

I often reflect on the debate of whether we are born with moral values or whether ethical codes are usually instilled in children by parents or caregivers. I've witnessed it with my own children, who will deliberately cause harm to one another or to one of our animals at home, and it reminds me of my frog killing when I was child.

Jon told me his parents weren't present in his early life, so without someone showing him what was right and what was wrong during those early stages of development, was his moral compass in some way skewed?

With almost one million children in South Africa living without both parents, and a further 10 million with an absent or dead father, the high crime rates are not surprising. Studies have shown that 'the absence of the father is the single most important cause of crime', according to a publication by the Office of Juvenile Justice and Delinquency Prevention in the United States. This may in part explain Jon's malevolence towards animals and his lack of consideration for the consequences of the many risks he was prepared to take to get rich quickly.

South Africa's history of violence and social engineering broke up families and undermined the social fabric of entire communities across the country, effectively depriving millions of people of loving parental guidance and proper education. While I certainly don't condone Jon's actions, a better understanding of why so many South Africans have become involved in poaching is just as important as deploying the drones, dogs and personnel to fight the crime.

The journey with Jon would never have happened if Renias and I did not have such a strong relationship. Renias trusted that I would not have Jon arrested and Jon believed Renias when he relayed that message to him. If it weren't for Renias's relationships within his community, he wouldn't have managed to persuade Jon to agree to come to Londolozi in the first place.

Looking back, I firmly believe Jon wanted to change his life. He was tired of running from the police but he didn't have the ability to fully transform himself. He didn't have the resources and support at his disposal to make a change for the long term, and perhaps needed counselling to tease out those deep fears that were pushing him to commit crimes.

Jon taught us that the process of 'rehabilitating' people involved in wildlife crime is far more complex than merely giving them a job or putting them on a training course. There is no single intervention, silver-lined solution to combating the poaching crisis. It starts with a stable, loving family unit followed by good-quality education, skills development and an attractive job opportunity driven by a growing economy.

Considering that we came to know Jon's life situation so well, we failed to develop a meaningful enough relationship with him that could withstand robust conversation and guidance, including psychological analysis, to assist him in making informed decisions to improve his life. Game reserve administrators are aware that poaching is a symptom of the social and moral crisis we are currently facing in this country, and indeed the world over.

People who witnessed the effort we all put into Jon often say that he betrayed us. I suppose it is true that he violated a contract, an informal and personal agreement that is unlikely to ever be repaired. But to counter the associated reactive emotions of anger, you need to examine objectively the factors that drove Jon to hunt illegally in the first place.

When I ask Renias about his thoughts on Jon, he says, 'Jon is like a lion, he has that instinct to live and kill like a predator. We should leave him alone now.'

The elusive nature of trust

The first time I wished Renias happy birthday, on his self-selected birthdate, he hardly acknowledged me. I later learnt that birthday celebrations are not really a part of his culture, and that he personally had no interest in observing the day. Because he doesn't know the exact date anyway, it holds little emotional significance for him.

In professional relationships, individuals inevitably hail from disparate language groups, upbringings and religious or spiritual beliefs and the culture we come from shapes us profoundly. Rarely do we all share the same world view.

There were occasions when I was dealing with an urgent matter at work and I addressed Renias without observing certain formalities. As is often the Western approach, I'd launch into an issue without necessarily acknowledging or greeting him fully. This annoyed him at first but he became accustomed to it when he realised it was part of my personality and perhaps also an influence from my culture. By the same token, I tried to make an effort to heed particular manners associated with his culture, such as a respectful greeting, being mindful of my tone when addressing him or being seated when he was. Over time, we found a compromise, a happy medium that worked for both of us.

Cultural differences often caused tension in the early years of our relationship. Over the years, while presenting to companies all over the country, I've seen this cultural dynamic play out in diverse teams and it has the potential to create resentment without one person even being aware of it. To avoid this happening with Renias, I needed to develop a stronger sense of personal power and it was vital for me to gain insights into his culture. I needed to immerse myself deeply and sincerely in an effort to develop a sense of acceptance of Renias's cultural idiosyncrasies. I wasn't satisfied observing only the superficial stuff, but wanted to gain a genuine and honest understanding of his culture and the behaviour associated with being respectful and respected.

Things worked well initially but an unravelling sometimes occurred when the pressures of work began to take effect. Basic communication is often touted as the panacea for effective team building and personal relationships, but it carries less weight in exchanges between people from separate language groups. Nothing should be taken for granted and at some point in the early stage of my association with Renias, I realised that I sometimes needed to check something with him in a respectful manner if I didn't have 100 per cent clarity on it. In some instances, the deciphering of a message delivered in plain English, or any other language for that matter, requires knowledge of the context and cultural undertone it comes from. To communicate effectively with someone of another language group, you need first to understand their culture, irrespective of what language you're speaking.

There have been times over the years when Renias and I simply did not gel, when things went wrong while we were out in the bush and that caused friction between us. Whether it be a disagreement about the plan for a game drive or me not paying attention to Renias while driving through thorn trees, we had our squabbles. Something that really irked Renias in the later years of our relationship was when I would ask him to be ready to travel somewhere without explaining what we were going to do, resulting in him once bringing his smart presentation suit jacket and shiny black shoes to a tracking job!

Leading a diverse team of people requires far more comprehensive communication than you might think, things such as details on your vision, the victories, failures and honest information on money matters, make people feel part of the team and its mission. We often had informal debriefs that helped to settle frivolous day-to-day matters but sometimes, usually due to extreme fatigue, we'd fail to address the minor issues and this would eventually compound in an eruption and we'd end up having a huge argument.

One winter I took a liking to the head ranger's ex-girlfriend, a foolish error in judgement that resulted in Renias and me being 'banished' to Londolozi's most southern camp. Tumbela, a Shangaan word that means 'hiding' was our base for six weeks. Poor Renias was exiled to Tumbela simply for his association with me. In hindsight, it was probably a good idea for me to 'hide away' for a while!

Tumbela only had four rooms and eight guests in total and was far from the social action of the main Londolozi camp. We earned far fewer tips; salt in the wound as far as I was concerned, but a clever move by the head ranger. The small camp was tucked away among tall, leafy boer-bean trees on the banks of the Msuthu River. It was the year 2000 and over 1 200 millimetres of rain had fallen that season and for the first time I saw the Sand River burst its banks. It raged so loudly that it was difficult to sleep at night and several lodges, including Sabi Sabi River Lodge, were washed away.

For weeks, we weren't able to receive any guests at the lodge because many of the roads had been washed away, including the one to the airstrip. The mosquito population exploded in the pools of water that had collected and many of us contracted malaria. The floods, which were followed by intense heat, resulted in the grass growing to unprecedented heights. On one of the first evening game drives after the rain, Renias spotted a lion lying in the tall grass in a clearing very close to the lodge. As we drove towards it, the long grass lapped over the bonnet of the Land Rover, throwing up clouds of tiny seeds that flew into our eyes. They were the worst conditions for someone like me with a grass-seed allergy and I eventually started to carry a bottle of antihistamine eye drops around with me. I reckon I could have sold that bottle for thousands, that's how desperate some people were to rid themselves of their red, itchy and swollen eyes.

Then there was a great proliferation of golden-orb spiders; thousands of massive yellow-and-black spiders emerged almost overnight. People developed instant arachnophobia after going on one game drive. The bush was full of spiderwebs that often hung across the road, so we either had to drive through them or underneath them. Often the spiders dropped into the vehicle, creating much consternation, so we spent more time avoiding spiders than actually looking for animals. We struggled to find animals anyway because the bush was so thick and most of the roads were too waterlogged to drive on, so it dramatically reduced our access to many parts of the game reserve. Driving off-road meant a high likelihood of getting stuck and it was frustrating for the guides and guests alike. The relentless rain, heat, humidity, mozzies, grass seeds, spiders and the scarcity of animals all created fertile ground for frayed nerves and conflict. Suffice to say, 2000 was a tough year all round.

I steered the vehicle off the road, while at the same time wiping grass seeds out of my eyes, and headed in the direction of the lion that Renias had spotted. About halfway across the clearing, the front wheels of the Land Rover suddenly fell away into a massive aardvark burrow concealed by the long grass. The force of the fall launched Renias off the tracker seat like a rocket and he flew forward, initially landing on his feet but stumbling under the momentum, and eventually tripping and falling and finally disappearing into the tall grass. It was like detonating a landmine and the grass erupted with 21 lions exploding from their grassy beds, growling, charging, lashing their tails and fleeing, all at the same time.

A South African guest, a manager from a steel company that was doing work at the lodge, shot to his feet and shouted, 'Julle voetsek!' to the lions. Someone else's nose was bleeding after bashing it on one of the roll-bars and this was all happening while Renias lay motionless on the ground watching the mayhem unfold around him. The guest with the nosebleed had his left index finger in his nostril to stem the flow of blood, while taking photos of the growling lions with his right hand! Fortunately, the lions left Renias unscathed and he stood up in reasonably good spirits. Especially considering he'd been deposited into the middle of the biggest pride of lions at Londolozi! It wasn't anyone's fault and the lions had been so well hidden lying flat in the high grass and I hadn't been driving too fast so no one was seriously injured. I looked back at Renias sitting with the guests in the back of the vehicle and I could see he was slightly rattled.

The next afternoon we set out with the same guests on their second evening drive. Meandering through a woodland, a dung beetle flew straight into Renias's left eye causing him to almost collapse off the front of the Land Rover. Dung beetles are renowned for their failed navigation systems and getting hit in the face at least once in the summer season is to be expected. Seeing Renias's reaction and not realising the pain he was in, I burst out laughing. Renias was not amused and sat in the back of the vehicle with his fleece wrapped around his head, saying nothing for the rest of the game drive. I secretly found that quite funny too!

When we stopped for the drinks break, he told me I had belittled him, a man thirteen years my senior, in front of our guests. I immediately apologised and while my automatic reflex was to laugh, I knew it would have offended him even more. Particularly considering what had happened the previous day with the pride of lions. I laughed at Renias at a stage in our relationship when I did not have the social standing to do so. Laughing at someone can be construed as an insult in any culture and as far as Renias was concerned you can laugh at your contemporaries or your friends, but it is downright disrespectful to do so at someone older than you. By this stage, it had started raining again so we headed back to the lodge in a sombre mood having not had many good sightings.

Later that night, I returned to the staff village after supper with the guests. I passed Renias's room and saw him and some building contractors sitting and having a few drinks around a fire. He didn't greet me. They were drinking marula beer, which can have either a very weak or a very strong alcohol content, depending on its state of fermentation, and I said something patronising to the effect of, 'Keep it tidy,' but he did not respond. As I was drifting off to sleep, I could hear Renias's voice getting progressively louder as he regaled everyone with story after story. They must be drinking the strong version of marula beer, I thought.

I woke at 3am and I could still hear Renias's voice, although far less coherently, and I remember feeling slightly irritated as I needed him to be on form the next day. We hadn't seen many animals with our guests and I needed us to make an extra effort for them. When I arrived at the lodge that morning to meet the guests for early morning coffee, Renias wasn't there. I knew why and so I tried to delay our departure by telling the guests an arbitrary story but I could see they were anxious to get going on the game drive – despite the spiders, grass seeds, humidity and all other manner of natural phenomena. Still no Renias. Feeling annoyed, I packed the hotbox with coffee and rusks, grabbed my rifle and headed out, sans Renias.

It was the first time I'd done that and it felt good. Renias had a habit of running late and I always waited for him. To compensate for his lateness, I would usually show the guests a few tracks in the car park as a means of buying him an extra few minutes but that day I was fed up and so I left him behind to prove a point. I told the guests he needed to see the doctor about his eye as an explanation for him not being there, which was a complete fabrication on my part. Fifteen minutes later a call came through on the radio and it was Renias: 'Majombane, come in. Come back to the lodge.'

Not wanting to create a scene in front of the guests, and assuming Renias's post-marula beer-binge state, I simply switched off the radio and continued with the drive. One of the Sabi Sabi guides found a cheetah on the common boundary so the guests and I spent the entire morning watching it and then drove back to camp feeling pretty good about myself. When we got back, Renias was waiting for us and he was seething. My indignation had irked him badly and he kept saying, 'I will find you, one day.' It was his way of saying he would get back at me or show me up in some way, one day.

He claimed he'd seen us drive out of the car park that morning and had shouted for me to stop. He was angry because I mistrusted his ability and I'd unilaterally decided that he wasn't going to be on time. He questioned me as to how I thought I could make that assessment, not least of all because he'd been waking up at dawn for two decades before even I arrived on the scene.

But he was too tired and too hungover to present much more of a fight so he repeated, 'I will find you, one day,' and wandered back to his room. I mistakenly thought that Renias now knew that I wouldn't wait for him if he was late in the future. Within a day or two, things settled at Tumbela, Renias's eye healed and we found our groove again. Or so I thought.

A month later, I attended a gathering for all the guides at one of the neighbouring lodges. I only went to the party after having supper in the boma, and I remember crawling into bed after a long night with the francolins calling, an indication that it was basically morning. I awoke to Renias shouting my name and telling me to wake up, 'Majombane! Vuka!' I vaulted out of bed onto the veranda of my room to discover that Renias had brought the entire complement of guests, in the Land Rover, to wake me up! He sat behind the steering wheel and grinned at me knowingly. It was the most embarrassing moment of my guiding career and was made even worse when a large German man teased me, 'Alex, I see you get a half hour more than we did!' Renias's revenge was complete.

In an intense work cycle of eight weeks, seven days a week and then two weeks off, I learnt many valuable lessons in how to conduct myself working in partnership with a person from a different culture. And, more importantly, how to avoid being viewed as just another arrogant young white guy showing no real interest or tolerance of another culture. Renias's reaction to my disrespect towards him in the lion and dung beetle incidents was exacerbated by a belief that he carried and a concept I knew nothing about – 'thakathi' or witchcraft. This is a practice whereby a spiteful person makes use of magic to inflict harm on someone else by using herbs and other medicines known as 'umuthi'. In the research I did on the topic, it is defined as 'the targeted application of negative energy used with the intention to harm or even kill a person'. Misfortune can be linked to angry ancestors and what I didn't know at the time was that the Shangaan people have a very strong relationship with their ancestors.

While Renias didn't think I was using witchcraft, he thought someone else might have been and this caused him, by his own admission, to become hypersensitive to events around him. Whether I believed it to not, or understood it or not, was irrelevant because Renias did. His run of bad luck and what he perceived as curious behaviour on my part, as I had not behaved that way before, gave him the sense that something was amiss. At the time, I gave it little attention when he explained it to me because I simply didn't believe in it. I thought that as long as it was a belief, it remained just that. It is something that is not known and is therefore merely a mental construct, and I arrogantly thought it was all hogwash.

Renias perceived my attitude as a rejection of his culture and of him in his personal capacity. He once even said to me, 'You like to undermine my culture,' in perfect English. It was a phrase that stopped me in my tracks. I didn't expect him to say that. For him, witchcraft is as real as the sun rising in the morning. He made it clear that if I was to remain in partnership with him, I needed to respect his beliefs without judging or criticising them. He didn't need me to believe it; he simply needed me to sincerely acknowledge that it was something that was real and important to him. That was all he expected.

Some years later, Renias and I were warned by a sangoma that we may be involved in a car accident in the future as evidently someone was jealous of our work. For the first time, I found myself paying careful attention to something I didn't understand or necessarily believe. The visit to the sangoma was an interesting experience and gave me a heightened sense of awareness of people's individual belief systems. It's easy to be dismissive of a belief when it has no direct impact on you but it is an entirely different matter when it involves you. In fact, a year later, I was involved in a car accident but too many drinks at the pub was a more plausible explanation than witchcraft!

An ecologically tragic belief, albeit one from a country far from South Africa, is having a devastating impact on our rhino. It's an entrenched and mystical belief that has existed for thousands of years and is sadly unlikely to change in the short term. Science has proved that rhino horn has no medicinal purpose but many Asian countries place great value on its efficacy. The consumption of rhino horn may have a powerful placebo effect on its users and much of it is consumed by people trying to cure cancer or reduce the symptoms of chemotherapy. One argument is that it is indeed a health crisis that is generating the demand in Asia. In countries such as Vietnam it's becoming increasingly common to use rhino horn as a status symbol to demonstrate success and wealth. Considering the cumulative demand of a vast Asian population, combined with a growing economy and no free press to educate the ignorant, it doesn't bode well for rhinos. However, all cultures in the world hold their own beliefs and carry out traditional practices that may appear strange to the outsider. Consider for a moment the First World idea that diamonds symbolise eternal love. Would people from Western cultures stop buying engagement rings for their fiancées if they knew the shocking human rights abuses against children, and the bloodshed associated with selling diamonds in many African countries? There is very little awareness in the market of where to purchase ethically sourced diamonds and some people don't really care to ask about the circumstances under which a diamond comes to be sold in a jewellery store. Consider the demise of the great rainforests and the impact on the atmosphere caused by humanity's voracious and excessive need to consume red meat. Westerners like to accuse Asians of social and environmental conflict but we are equally complicit.

A few years after my lesson in witchcraft, while walking in a village bordering the Kruger Park, I was approached by a villager who claimed I was a 'rich guy' because I worked in the game reserve. He was alluding to the vast opportunity the reserve offered to become involved in the highly lucrative rhino horn trade.

I told Renias that I was concerned about the relationship fallout between the people trying to protect the reserves and those accused of poaching, many of whom lived in the surrounding villages. Considering South Africa's social history, it is understandable that community leadership tends to protect the interests of people living in villages. People from the local villages were being called in for questioning and some were even being roughed up in the process. A few young men had been shot and killed by anti-poaching operatives, having a further negative impact on the relationship between the game reserve and its neighbours. Many of the private reserves, as well as the Kruger National Park, had done excellent work in developing facilities, schools, clinics and, of course, providing job opportunities, and I was concerned the goodwill, trust and relationships would be undermined by the rhino-poaching crisis.

The situation was brought even closer to home when some of the people implicated in rhino poaching and aiding the criminals lived in the villages close to Renias and were known to us. At the same time, Renias started to receive numerous calls on his cellphone while we were out tracking in the bush. I was used to his wife calling him at all hours about all manner of things – their children, transport issues, people's requests for favours – but something felt different about these calls.

Firstly, Renias spoke English on these calls, which was unusual because he usually spoke Shangaan when people phoned him. I started to wonder whether a poaching syndicate had been in contact with him. Had they recruited him? Were they asking him for information about the whereabouts of rhino in the game reserve?

I didn't want to pry into Renias's affairs but I had a burning need to question him about the calls he was receiving. My mind was racing with thoughts of Renias's possible involvement in rhino poaching. He is known by so many people in the local villages as an expert tracker and a person who knows the landscape better than most. He knew where the rhinos grazed, their territorial scent-marking sites and their movements, so it would be a simple exercise for him to poach the rhino himself or accurately guide someone else to shoot one. And, worst of all, because some of the alleged poachers lived in neighbouring villages they had easy access to Renias during his off time.

I continued to ask myself whether Renias, someone who has dedicated his life to wildlife and who understands its intrinsic value, could really be a candidate to be a poacher. These thoughts occupied my mind for weeks. Because the acts of a poacher are driven mostly by the need for money and Renias was well established in a good job, I didn't think he needed the money. This made me feel slightly better and despite all my thoughts and the coincidences I'd decided there were, I resolved to leave the matter alone. It was too sensitive. I wasn't sure of any of the facts and by broaching the subject with him, I risked him misconstruing that I was accusing him. An accusation like that was a serious matter for anyone working in the game reserve and I wasn't prepared to jeopardise our relationship based on the vague and incidental ideas I had in my head. I trusted Renias's technical competence in the bush, but for the first time I began to question whether I trusted his nature.

A few months later, Renias and I were conducting a trailing assessment in a group with one of our students from the academy. At the time, we were running the academy from Londolozi and both staying on the property, but no longer working there. We found a rhino bull's track next to a dam that we then asked the student to follow. The assessment tests a student's ability to find a suitable track, accurately age it and then follow the trail until the rhino is found. Along the way, the student must demonstrate their ability to recognise the animal's tracks on the ground and anticipate its movements. Depending on how far the animal moves, the assessment can take up to five hours to complete.

Each Tracker Academy student is assessed once a month over the course of the year's training programme. That day, the rhino bull's track was over a day old, making for a good test of a student's trailing ability. The trail led us away from the dam into a woodland where we found evidence of where the animal had rested. There had been some light drizzle the night before so the student was struggling to stay on the trail as the tracks had been partially obscured by the rain. He regularly lost the spoor but was doing reasonably well to predict the rhino's direction of movement and we pressed on slowly. The morning was warming as the sun got higher and as I adjusted my cap, something caught my attention up ahead: a vulture landing in a tree a few hundred metres in front of us. Perhaps a leopard kill, I thought.

At this point, Renias stopped the student and asked him to explain what he thought the rhino was doing and in what direction it had possibly gone. By now the student had lost the tracks completely so Renias pointed out a partial print of the rhino's track that the student had missed. In an attempt to assist him, Renias pointed out a conspicuous impression of the broad middle toenail of the track. Renias always loves his quick explanations and demonstrations to help students see and understand the trail.

In the two minutes of conversation that ensued, a dozen vultures started settling in the trees and I made the suggestion to break from the rhino tracks and investigate the vulture activity. The hissing and squealing calls made by squabbling vultures feeding on a carcass could easily be heard. As we got closer, Renias spotted something that made my blood run cold. In a small clearing, a dead rhino lay on its stomach, with both its horns cut off. Its eyes had already been pecked out by a bateleur eagle and a single hyaena was feeding on the meat between the rhino's hindquarters. The hyaena saw us and bolted and we stood speechless for a few moments. The students wanted to get closer but because it was the scene of a crime, we needed to preserve all the evidence.

As we stood there, I was struck by the reality of the situation: the power of money and status, elements so sought after by most human beings, were motivating South Africans, through a misplaced dream, to kill a rhino with the lure of it changing their life forever. How do you fight that? On the one hand, there is the ever-growing and affluent Asian market, while on the other hand, there are desperately poor people with the means and access to supply that rhino horn. The result is that close to 9 000 rhinos have been killed in South Africa since 2008. All of them butchered in the name of a questionable belief system that has no link to Africa whatsoever.

The rest of that day was spent providing statements to the police, who seemed completely desensitised to the sight of another poached rhino. Whoever was responsible for the murder of that old bull remains a mystery and I'm doubtful the police ever arrested anyone in connection with it. Seeing that dead rhino was as emotionally confronting for me as the day Eric took his life. I felt like I'd lost a dear friend. The person who killed that magnificent animal was devoid of any ethical code, certainly from a conservation perspective, and I was reminded of the dire need for trackers to be professionally trained in the moral principles associated with living and working in nature.

THE ELUSIVE NATURE OF TRUST

In the following months and years, rhino carcasses were discovered on a daily basis in the greater Kruger National Park. At one point some scientists were of the view that more rhino were being killed annually than there were rhino calves being born. The beginning of a local extinction was becoming a real possibility. As I write this chapter, my phone beeps with a message from a friend informing me of twenty rhinos found poached, in a single day, in a game reserve.

We were never sure whether there were poaching gangs active in the reserve but the anti-poaching staff told me that the number of incursions into the park was increasing on a monthly basis and gun battles were taking place weekly in some parts. We received a lot of enquiries from security companies wanting to deploy some of our tracker graduates to anti-poaching units in an attempt to bolster the protection efforts.

At a conference I presented at around this time, one of the delegates asked how I could be sure that our tracker graduates were not being trained as future poachers. My response was that it was no different to the way IT graduates could make use of their skills to hack banking computer systems, if they wanted to. That answer was understandably insufficient but I really didn't have an alternative response. All I could do was work harder to ensure that the correct ethical code was being rigorously installed in our tracker students.

The point remains that trackers possess the skills to successfully track and find rhinos and it is a risk the industry has to try to mitigate. Since 2012 we have placed a lot more focus on conservation ethics at Tracker Academy in an attempt to facilitate a greater understanding of animal rights and the physical, spiritual and psychological benefits associated with healthy ecosystems and wild places. Long-time mentor and member of Tracker Academy family, Dr Ian McCallum, psychiatrist, author and former guide, spends one-on-one time with all of our students to emphasise and discuss the ethical behaviour in the conservation industry. I firmly believe Ian's work is making a difference to our students' outlook and is prompting them to pass on their knowledge in an effort to educate everyone they come into contact with. Peer pressure is an underrated factor influencing young men and if Tracker Academy can produce graduates who exhibit a strong sense of personal leadership and environmental awareness, it represents another layer of protection of our heritage.

I was struggling to reconcile my seemingly fragile belief in Renias's love of nature with all the coincidences that had taken place, and it gave power to my concern that he might, in some way, be involved in rhino poaching. I still had not confronted him about the issue as I simply had nothing material to base a conversation on. But late one night, I received a call from Londolozi's security manager who told me that Renias had been briefly apprehended and questioned following a situation where he was caught driving a vehicle that had allegedly been used in a rhino-poaching incident. My worst nightmare had come true; all my concerns and questions around Renias's involvement now seemed completely justified and I felt powerless. I'd spent two decades with the man and I was now questioning whether I actually knew him at all. I thought he loved animals and I'd personally witnessed him connect on an emotional level with animals, so none of this made sense. Was his compassion for nature all just a show? I immediately thought back to the journey we had had with Jon and how it obviously hadn't been internalised for Renias, even though he'd witnessed, first hand, how Jon had ruined his own life.

The incident represented high stakes for us as everything Renias and I had worked for seemed uncertain, and, in fact, appeared to be on the brink of complete collapse. Images of all the donors to our academy flashed through my mind; they would be distraught to hear this had happened. I immediately headed up to Renias's house after speaking to the security manager for a while, and decided it was time for us to have a robust conversation. When I arrived at his door, I could see he was shaken by the treatment he had received from the anti-poaching guards. He had been treated like a criminal and it must have been awful for him to experience. I went inside and he sat on his bed while I sat on his handmade wooden chair and we started to talk.

He explained that one of his family members had asked him to drive the vehicle from Dixie back to the game reserve. That was it. Nothing illegal was found in the vehicle and so I pushed him for details about the strange phone calls he'd been receiving. He explained that he'd been speaking to a mechanic who had been fixing his car and didn't speak Shangaan. I kept asking questions and tried as best as I could to avoid an accusatory tone of questioning.

Then Renias said to me, 'Buti, I will volunteer to take a polygraph test and they can ask me anything they like.' I instantly felt calm. Did he know that a polygraph test is only 90 per cent accurate, though? What happens if he did poorly on the test because he was too nervous? I wasn't sure how to respond to his statement and found myself wanting to protect him. In the end, we agreed taking a test was the right thing to do and a few weeks later he took the test and passed flawlessly.

Although I had always trusted Renias's technical ability, for some reason I hadn't trusted his character. If trust of character is defined by intent and integrity I didn't know what his intentions were and therefore doubted his integrity. But why? Renias had never given me a reason not to trust his character.

Am I just an untrusting person? Maybe. Were my thoughts influenced by racial bias? Definitely. My thoughts and presumptions were directly influenced by the image I had conjured of a black guy living in a poor rural community apparently harbouring alleged rhino poachers. That was all my subconscious needed to create a clear version of a story, even though none of it was based on any real fact. It was a tale I had told myself and one that had the potential to ruin a twenty-plus year relationship. It's clear to me now that not trusting Renias created a bigger risk and threat to our partnership than trusting him would have, but this was a counterintuitive thought I did not consider in the midst of the events.

I had firmly believed Renias and I were in a high-trust relationship but I realised I wasn't so sure I had really trusted him at all. In a relationship where there is true trust, difficult conversations can be had despite one person perhaps stating something factually incorrect; the other person still gets the meaning without misinterpreting the overall message.

Renias and I should have had that conversation long before

the anti-poaching crew got to him. I had confused my trust of his ability with my trust of his character. We needed to inspire trust in each other again by talking openly and honestly to each other all the time and delivering the message with respect and complete transparency. I realised that my prejudicial thoughts were far more entrenched than I chose to acknowledge and I was fortunate that Renias had the wherewithal and strength of character to confront the matter in a bold and forthright manner. He took a risk in choosing to undergo a polygraph test and the fact that he was comfortable for me to write and talk about the incident further demonstrates his self-assurance. There's no doubt that the poaching issue, combined with our years of time together, has resulted in greater willingness to tackle the difficult conversations more effectively.

As of 2018, published rhino-poaching statistics reveal a drop in the number of rhinos killed since 2015. Whether the numbers are accurate or not, as there is no formal data to support them, is not clear but many of my colleagues who work tirelessly every single day to protect rhinos inform me that the number of incursions is actually growing.

In the Sabi Sands Game Reserve the number of incursions and actual killings of rhinos has dropped by 96 per cent since 2016. This result follows the efforts of a project called Connect Conservation, a collaboration between the tech companies, Cisco and Dimension Data, to create smart fences that allow early detection of poachers and accurate reporting. With the help of a committed warden and his staff, this proactive, somewhat disruptive, security solution has allowed the rhinos to roam freely in a safe haven.

There's no single intervention that can protect endangered wildlife. For Renias and me, providing environmental education to the community members concerned is the most important factor. We have witnessed many graduates of Tracker Academy return to their communities and play an impactful role in inspiring their peers. This makes us believe that relevant education is a powerful force for conservation and is a motivation for us to keep teaching.

The path of a tracker

I've never felt like a 'natural' at anything in my life. I always had to put in more hours than my peers at school, both in my studies as well as on the sports field. Looking back, I realise the great boredom I experienced as a result of having to work really hard at things contributed to my mediocrity. As a boy, I regularly pondered the purpose of school and I possessed almost no ability to motivate myself to be excellent at anything. My arrival at Londolozi, however, and being immersed in a life of animals and wildlife and people I could relate to, kindred spirits who understood me, sparked an enormous sense of inspiration within me.

For the first ten years of being a guide and environmental manager, I was in a state of deep personal and professional satisfaction but as the years passed and my experience grew, I became aware that I was stagnating. Adding to this feeling of stagnation was that I was constantly being urged by friends and guests, who seemingly had successful lives and businesses, that I should go back to the 'real world' and get a 'real job' where I would earn a proper living and could then start a family. Guiding is often compared to being a ski instructor; do it for a while, have a great experience, meet lots of people and then move on.

I was told that I shouldn't leave it too late as 'you're not getting any younger', a comment I heard countless times. This societal expectation appeared to be the norm and a social construct that actually made a lot of sense to me at that time in my life. I started to believe I was living in a heavenly jail with no options available to me to improve myself. A place where beyond the game reserve's boundaries there existed fewer and fewer professional opportunities the longer I stayed.

In a deeply confused state, I asked Dave Varty for a month's sabbatical for the time and space I needed to try to figure out my next life move. I was also dealing with heartbreak, having recently had a girlfriend break up with me and start dating one of the other guides, which was adding to the intensity of my feelings at the time. Sitting in his boma the night before I departed, Dave offered me a cricket analogy saying I was 'like a talented fast bowler who didn't want to bowl'. No one had ever told me I was talented before and Dave's comment left me feeling even more perplexed and confused.

I decided to travel to Peru, and once I got there, I drove over the Andes mountain range through the cloud forest and eventually emerged onto the banks of the mighty Amazon River. I was struck by the power of the gigantic body of water and its presence and quiet magnificence. Having left South Africa just 24 hours before, I was in the middle of the Amazon jungle in Manu National Park, where the vibrancy of animal and bird life was dazzling. Like all unspoilt wilderness areas, it invoked a reverence in me, unique to wild places.

I soon discovered that the sandy beaches of the great river were perfect for reading tracks, and before our group even reached the camp for the night, I was on the trail of a jaguar. Jaguars are similar in colour and camouflage to leopards but they are bigger and are found only in the remote regions of South and Central America, especially in the Amazon basin. That evening, I stood on the riverbank and watched the water flow past silently yet so powerfully. A log drifted past and caught my gaze and drew on my awareness, and in an exhausted, strangely jet-lagged moment of clarity, I understood that the log was in the perfect place, travelling at the perfect speed and heading in the perfect direction, courtesy of the river.

After a soul-searching month in South America, I returned to Londolozi with a sense of renewed focus and intent. I'd set aside any thoughts of moving to the city or going back to the 'real world' or switching professions. I realised I'd gained valuable skills as a naturalist and tracker in my time at Londolozi and I wanted to push those skills as far as I could and build on them further.

It was at this time that Dave tasked me with managing the environmental department at Londolozi, with the proviso that as long as I met and superseded the environmental outcomes incumbent upon me, I was free to craft a vocation mutually beneficial to Londolozi and me. I'd learnt an enormous amount from Renias in the years we had already worked together and I wanted to test those skills. I wanted to put my skills through an objective system of peer review.

I'd heard about an organisation that evaluated trackers in South Africa and issued certificates endorsed by the Field Guides Association of Southern Africa (FGASA). At the time, the existing tracking certificates included tracker level 1, 2, 3 and Senior Tracker. There was also a master tracker certificate awarded to those who Louis Liebenberg, the originator of the evaluation system, deemed to have made novel contributions to the field of tracking.

The evaluations comprised the identification of animal tracks and signs and the skill of following an animal's trail. The three tracker levels were based on percentage scores for both disciplines and the assessment system was a perfect way of testing skills. To attain a Senior Tracker qualification, you had to score 100 per cent for both components and because of this requirement, there were only nine certified Senior Trackers in South Africa at the time.

The tests were entirely practical and included tracks and signs with 40 to 50 questions, each weighted in respect of the level of difficulty. The track questions ranged from insects to birds to antelope and to elephants. Candidates are rewarded for answering complex questions correctly and penalised for answering easy questions incorrectly. Candidates then have to find a fresh track of one of the Big Five, make a decision on the track's age and suitability to follow and then trail the animal until it is found. Elements such as the tracker's knowledge of track age, number of animals present, speed of movement, general awareness, ability to recognise tracks and anticipate movement, to predict dangerous situations, and finally, to find the animal without it being aware of the tracker's presence are all yardsticks for completion. It is no easy feat when dealing with nature's multitude of uncontrollable elements and variables!

Renias and I had already subjected ourselves to the various tests in order to qualify as official trackers and so we were certified as Tracker level 3, although, unofficially, Renias was a far superior tracker. The big prize was Senior Tracker and we committed ourselves with vigour to fulfilling its requirements.

Part of the testing process meant we had to travel to other game reserves, where the slightly unfamiliar terrain provided a surprising mental challenge that needed to be overcome. Although the same animals occurred in these reserves, the 'away game' seemed to drain me of my confidence. Sleeping in a strange bed, being with unfamiliar people, eating different food and experiencing different conditions all contributed to that universal phenomenon of performing better when on home turf. Renias seemed far less perturbed and he managed to pass the senior track and sign part of his test on his second attempt, and the trailing component on his first. At that stage only one person had ever passed both components of the senior evaluation on their first attempt and that was Renias's older brother, Phineas Mhlongo.

I failed the track and sign evaluation three times and eventually passed it on my fourth attempt. The track of a white-tailed mongoose was my nemesis; it caused me to fall short on three occasions as I developed a mental block around a slightly obscure example of a white-tailed mongoose track, and kept confusing it with a jackal, or the other way around. The tracks are similar in the general shape and size but my failure to distinguish them from one another tormented me for months after.

Having finally passed the track and sign evaluation, I progressed to the trailing component. I failed the test once and decided to commit to improving my trailing skills by practising on my own in the bush whenever I got the chance. I started trailing lions at every given opportunity and I recall visiting the environmental team at a site where they were laying a water pipe, when I noticed the tracks of a few lions crossing the road. I trailed them for several hours until I was successful in finding them. In summer, I'd rise before dawn to track lions and I would then be at the office by 6:45am when the team met to discuss the day's tasks. Instead of taking any leave, I tracked every day. If there was a lion that walked on the Londolozi reserve at that time, I was probably behind it.

I had no clever training strategy other than to follow lion trails and then push myself to recognise their tracks and anticipate their movements, especially in places where tracks were not easily discernible. Like all cats, lions are soft-footed and can be challenging to trail, especially if there's only one of them to find whereas in a pride with several members they're a little easier to follow. However, if they're hunting they have a tendency to split up and go in different directions, complicating the tracking effort.

After a while I found a pattern whereby single territorial males usually walked in predictable directions, either patrolling their territory or looking to reunite with their pride, which made them slightly easier to track. A group of lionesses, by contrast, either represented the easiest trail if they were moving together along natural game paths with a particular intention of going somewhere, or they produced the most complex problem if they were hunting. They stalk, circle, chase and double back on themselves and that unpredictability forced me to think more deeply about their behaviour, where the prey was and what their motive was. Simply following a hunting lioness, track for track, without knowing the big picture, is exceptionally challenging, and I learnt more about lion behaviour in those six months of 'lone' tracking than in my entire guiding career.

Eventually the day came for my second attempt at the trailing component of the evaluation and, by extension, the full Senior Tracker qualification. Louis Liebenberg decided to conduct my evaluation at Londolozi, which did a lot to reduce my nervousness. We drove west from the Londolozi camp and stopped next to a small waterhole known as Guarri Pan, where I noticed evidence of a single lioness. I could see the tracks were reasonably fresh but I was concerned that committing to a lone lioness would present a particularly difficult trail for me to follow. I had no option, though; I could hardly ask the evaluators to look for a friendlier lion trail! Renias's brother, Elmon, who had recently qualified as Senior Tracker, accompanied Louis and me in the capacity of observer and local expert and co-evaluator.

'Good luck, mfo,' said Elmon as I hauled my tracking stick off the Land Rover and climbed off. I could feel my nerves and I sensed I needed some good fortune so I was pleased to get his encouragement. I first scouted the area for a few minutes to establish the lioness's direction. I desperately needed her to be going east or north as I knew that landscape intimately and it was also where the sandy soils were more conducive to seeing tracks. A southerly direction would also have been doable but not as good as east or north. West would be the worst outcome as the terrain there changed to the clayey black cotton soil, hard and dark, similar to the habitat where Renias grew up.

The lioness's tracks crossed the road in front of me directly north of Guarri Pan and I started to trail her. Within five minutes of following her, she had changed her bearing and was heading directly west. This was the worst possible start and my uncle Philip's often-mentioned words of advice, 'It's not about what happens to you but what you do about it,' which had become something of a mantra for me at this time of my life, came into my head. I had no option but to keep trying. The lioness's tracks then crossed a road, Elmon's Kraal, named after an old man who used to live in the area, and I stopped there to have a good look at the condition of the tracks at that point. Another Land Rover had driven over her tracks, partially obscuring them and depositing a lot of dust onto them.

I carried on walking up the road for a few metres and discovered the tracks of another lioness. Two lionesses was a small gift, I thought to myself. The lionesses were walking about 10 metres away from each other, in parallel, and heading in the same direction. I was pretty sure I'd tracked the two lionesses in the same general area on one of my lone training sessions, and that gave me a sense of confidence. I was buoyed by this and I started to trail with good momentum and, for the time being, I felt good.

The trail then entered a woodland of long and drying grass where it was clear a host of other animals had spent the night. I'd just started to develop some sort of flow when the track totally disappeared. I looked up ahead but couldn't find anything so I decided to play it safe and return to my last confirmed piece of evidence; a track superimposed on a buffalo dropping. I considered whether the lions were following the buffalo but I knew these lionesses and they were not known for hunting buffalo. I progressed painstakingly slowly for a few metres and was able to recognise another faint track, still heading west. Earlier that morning, while drinking my coffee, I'd heard lions calling a long way to the west and I wondered whether these lionesses were on their way to meet up with the rest of their pride.

I pressed on, cognisant that I shouldn't get myself too caught up in the detail if the evidence wasn't reliably there and so I made a mini prediction of where the trail was headed. This was my first attempt at anticipating the lionesses' movements and is a part of the evaluation the evaluators are very critical of in a Senior Tracker test. I walked on a bearing I thought was the right one, and when I came upon a clear game path with open soil, I saw no tracks. My prediction of their direction of movement was wrong and I started to doubt myself. I began to question whether the tracks were even that fresh. Had the vehicle that had driven over the tracks perhaps travelled the previous afternoon? A feeling of dread filled my body and I found myself fundamentally re-examining and querying my original hypothesis and it caused me to hesitate.

What would Renias have done in this scenario? I ran over the events so far and remembered the feeling I'd had upon finding that lioness's track, that familiar excitement whenever I saw a nice fresh lion track. I must be right, I thought. Speculating on a feeling was perhaps an imperfect approach and I was possibly grasping at straws. Maybe I'd never been very good at accurately ageing tracks, I said to myself. So many thoughts were running through my head, which were causing confusion and distracting me from the task at hand.

In an attempt to re-centre myself, I reminded myself that the last confirmed lion track I had seen had been heading up the slope towards the crest so I tentatively proceeded that way. I started thinking about how much fun I'd had practising my tracking skills over the last few months, and how this evaluation embodied the complete opposite. The test's anxiety construct was in full gallop and it was causing me to question my every decision. If I was going to succeed I had to find a way to calm myself and focus. Thoughts such as 'I need to pass this' and 'What will I say to people if I fail?' were racing through my mind and were thwarting my ability to perform.

When I had been practising alone in the bush, I never had any of those thoughts and had never doubted myself, and consequently I was able to express myself freely in my ability to follow the tracks. I found some calmness within myself by consciously substituting all the limiting self-judgements I was making with one clear thought, 'I will find.' It was an old mantra of Renias's that brought feelings of familiarity and freedom, feelings that had been eluding me up to this point.

If Renias had been there, he would've backed his ability to recognise a track up ahead in the knowledge that he'd made the correct decision and was headed in the right direction. I consciously made the decision to do the same. I surmised that there was nothing to suggest that the lions would suddenly change their direction. The vegetation had opened up so they would have had good visibility, providing no cause for any impulsive behaviour. I decided to stay the course and remain on the same trajectory. As I neared the crest, I noticed a termite mound just ahead and made the assumption that the lionesses would have either lain on the bare sand surrounding the mound, or used it as a vantage point to scan for prey. As I got 10 metres away, I could already see the lions had been there, and the sight of those pug marks may have been the most excited I've ever felt to see a lion track! I ferreted around the mound for a few moments and saw where the lions had continued west.

I had to believe the evaluators were impressed with my successful prediction as it had been a good few hundred metres with no evidence and they must have started doubting me. I felt a sense of a mini victory. That termite mound represented so much more than simply a termite mound and my confidence went up a few notches. The tracks then headed back into the grass, but now I was less concerned about seeing every track and was content to anticipate, with greater assurance this time, that I was on the right track. I saw a small herd of wildebeest grazing in the valley below and a few minutes later I saw where one of the lionesses had tread on top of a wildebeest track. I was now convinced the tracks were fresh and that I was on the right trail and that certainty within me further bolstered my confidence.

As I progressed slowly westwards, the substrate started to change, forming the dark, hard clay that I had been concerned about. But by that stage of the trail I'd developed more certainty and momentum, and although I lost the track periodically, it had less of a technical and emotional hold over me. I then found where the lionesses had rested and I was convinced that I'd closed the gap somewhat. My fear had largely disappeared and was replaced by a feeling of joyous synergy. I had come to a point where I cared less about the outcome and was just enjoying walking along this wild trail I was on. I felt immensely privileged and for a moment I couldn't fathom why I had doubted myself, or my choices in my life and career.

The sun was getting hotter and higher and it was a drier than usual February, so I knew the lions wouldn't be moving for much longer. I pressed on through the long grass down towards the dry riverbed at the bottom of the valley. I acknowledged to myself that the tracking conditions had become infinitely more difficult as the morning progressed but this did little to stop my progress. All I had to corroborate the presence of the lionesses' trail was small intermittent patches of black clay. I glanced back at the evaluators and saw Elmon staring into the grass and giving Louis the thumbs up. Which I took to mean, 'He's still on them.'

This was a difficult trail, with lots of stop-starts but I had found a rhythm. A transition began and I started to flow in the same way a cricketer sees the ball large and the game slows down. I started to move faster on the trail and when I lost it, I would invariably cut the tracks up ahead on a lone patch of soil or on one of the many game paths. I started to see the trail clearly in the long grass, where I had struggled initially. My decision-making became more and more accurate as the trail unfolded and I felt like I was deeply aware of the lions' movements.

I forgot about the evaluators' eyes on me and I was in sync with the lions, following on their secret trail through the most magnificent wilderness. By now it was sweltering but I had no thought of water, food or anything outside of me, other than what was happening in that moment. I could not feel the ticks on my legs that I noticed were bothering the evaluators and under my focused concentration, I felt pure magnetic joy. As the hours went by, my intensity did not subside and in many ways I felt I was at the nexus of my life's calling.

The skills I had spent years practising, all the time I had spent with Renias, the early days with Eric and his brutal death and all the failures and uncertainties of my childhood emboldened me at that point. I'd been forced to develop a sense of tenacity at certain moments in my life and this had helped me to get to this exact time and place. Every shaping moment that had broken me down had also re-formed me and it was all there, manifesting in that lion trail. Life had compelled me to walk my own path and I was on the trail of a lion, becoming someone I realised I'd always wanted to be. I was expressing myself in the spiritual act of tracking and it was less about the skill and more to do with the people, the events and the failures that had moulded me.

Back on the trail a while later, we arrived at a dam situated well west of Londolozi's western boundary and some 4 or 5 kilometres from our starting point. Because of the good relationship Londolozi has with Singita Game Reserve, we were permitted to track over the boundary and through their land. I found where the lionesses had drunk water and I could see the fresh droplets at the water's edge, as they'd turned away from their drink. I knew I was moments behind the lionesses.

The trail then led me west into a clearing with very short grass, where it was almost impossible to see the tracks. I looked up and saw a shady woodland beyond and had a strong sense the lions were resting there. I decided to leave the tracks altogether and in one last risky attempt to predict their movement, I walked up the clearing, and as I came around a small isolated thicket, I saw both lionesses lying in the grass. I snapped my fingers and gestured to the evaluators who were a few metres behind me. Elmon smiled proudly and congratulated me saying, 'Buti, Renias will be happy.'

Back at camp later that day, I was called to a debrief and feedback meeting and I was told I had passed the test. Apparently I was the youngest person at that time to achieve the distinction of Senior Tracker. I knew in my heart that it hadn't been perfect but I'd obviously done enough and I don't think I'd ever felt so fulfilled within myself. I fell asleep that night with a smile on my face and thought of that log drifting down the Amazon River. Everything was as it was meant to be. It was all perfect.

Reflecting on that day, the energy, focus and clarity that I had been able to access was far more important than receiving the actual accolade. The material achievement of attaining that certificate was merely a by-product of performing honed skills with momentum and doing exactly what I was supposed to do. I began to see tracking as less of a skill and more as a way of life. As a means to gain a connection with the deep-seated elements of our psyche that we seldom experience. A means to connect most profoundly with nature and to express our creative self.

Tracking introduced me to the notion of being present and

living in constant creative response to the tracks of life. To be open to opportunity, not in a commercial sense, but in alignment with my deepest, truest desires. The difference between an internal knowledge of being on track versus being told or influenced in terms of what to do or where to go. There was only one trail that day – the two lionesses I was following – and to succeed I'd had to find a way to stay on track, to stay on my trail. I've met so many people in life who are half-heartedly pursuing someone else's track, causing them to live in a miserable state of being.

Too much focus on the technical aspects has the potential to kill the inherent fascination that many people have for wildlife tracking. In some circles, trackers have become associated with identification, making it boring and seemingly unattainable. At the same time, an overly creative approach without the technical footing, such as the example of the people in California holding their hands over the track claiming they could 'see' what the animal was doing, potentially undermines tracking as a legitimate skill. Once sound foundational knowledge is in place, creativity can be nurtured by deliberately exposing yourself to new tracking problems.

The metaphor of tracking is a powerful one. We are all born trackers – tracking our families, the weather, our physical condition, our emotions, the stock markets, or a subtle new behaviour trait of a friend or colleague. Subliminally, we are constantly seeking evidence to survive, as well as to succeed and prosper. One of the problems with modern society is that we've become too passive, overly reliant on instructions, signposts, technology and a myriad intuitive digital directives that have undermined our natural inclination to seek. Apart from the excitement of tracking lions, I have grown interested in the process of tracking, whether it be tracking a wild animal, our emotions or a business deal.

We live in times when the focus is almost exclusively on the goal rather than on the manner in which we get there; where the process of life seems less important than the product of its labours. Adopting the mentality of a tracker allows our natural intelligence to emerge through quiet awareness. It is astonishing what life sometimes brings when you are on your own track.

The realisation of a dream

Over the years, Renias and I tracked different animals in a variety of locations in Africa and other parts of the world. It became clear that our collective skillset was unique and well developed, and we were keen to teach others. Many of the guides at Londolozi enviously voiced how lucky I was to work with Renias and so when I became the environmental manager, the guides flocked to Renias to work with him. I was thrilled that he was receiving the attention and recognition he deserved. He had developed a reputation, not only as a competent tracker, but someone whose love for nature is unquestionable.

Renias's presence on the tracker's seat radiated large and, for the guests, his energy was as enthralling as the leopards. Few people would forget that their tracker had it been Renias Mhlongo. He loved his work and at the same time he never stopped learning. To this day, it's not unusual to see Renias paging through his tattered old tree book in an attempt to identify a species he doesn't know. And this is after 35 years of working full time as a tracker. Most of the guides I know put down their books in year three!

I have always believed that we need more people like Renias, people who are as skilled but, more importantly, as committed to nature conservation as he is. As I had visited Dixie several times over the years, I had formed a relationship with many of the younger boys in the village. I was keen to engage with them as they were what I deemed to be the next generation of trackers. I was, however, surprised to learn that most of the youngsters were either not interested in tracking at all or had nowhere suitable to practise their skills.

Although Dixie is situated on a productive piece of wildlife estate, few naturally occurring animals inhabit the land any more. Only goats and cattle are found grazing the land as all other animals have slowly been harvested. In South Africa, the traditional means of an elder teaching a young person about bushcraft and animal tracking has sadly all but vanished. Renias and his three brothers were among the last to receive this indigenous knowledge from their father. Renias and I agreed that the only way to try to restore the dying art of tracking was to formalise its training, and so we started to put plans in place to open a specialist tracker training school.

A few years later, I resigned from Londolozi to pursue our dream to make a living from an ancient art few people even knew about. An acquaintance from the city once let it slip that she thought I

THE REALISATION OF A DREAM

was a 'trucker', and I spent my time driving trucks; that is how unknown tracking was! The realisation that I was going into the chilly wind of unemployment, to follow a vision that I had no certainty would materialise, was terrifying. I'd enjoyed the comforts of a monthly salary and endless US-dollar tips for many years and by the time I exited the Londolozi gates, I had no idea how I was going to survive.

All I knew was that I wanted to track wild animals. Quite why I decided to leave one of the best places on earth you can track animals, to go and track animals, didn't make sense but something was driving me that I couldn't articulate at the time. Being a tracker means living by your wits and being open and aware of things happening around you, so perhaps that's one of the reasons I decided I needed to leave Londolozi.

Something powerful yet intangible was pulling me to take a leap of faith into the unknown, and although I didn't know the details, I knew it had something to do with animals, tracking and rural people. I was only beginning to realise the power of the lessons tracking had taught me over the years. I was also about to learn that being a tracker doesn't necessarily mean following animals.

I drove out of the Londolozi boom gate feeling cautiously hopeful about the prospects of setting up and choosing my own track in life. As Renias once said to me, 'You must follow the signs if you want to find something.' These words were among my final thoughts as I left the game reserve.

Renias and I aimed to persuade someone to support our idea of starting a tracker school. We travelled all over the country meeting with as many people as we could, including conservation NGOs and numerous companies' corporate social responsibility departments. 'You guys are sure burning leather,' said an American friend of ours when we told him how many people we'd pitched to. But we had no success and so we decided to head to the United States to try to secure funding. We sold our services by teaching tracking in order to fund the trip.

We went to Yellowstone National Park in Wyoming where we tracked grizzly bears and wolves with Dr Jim Halfpenny and Meghan Walla-Murphy, two well-known American trackers. Of all the animals Renias and I had ever tracked, grizzlies are potentially the most dangerous. They are considered to be one of the most intelligent animals in North America and females with cubs, if provoked, will not hesitate to attack a human. Sadly, a little girl had been killed near Yellowstone the week before we arrived. We heard many stories from our American hosts about the danger grizzlies posed, so we were on high alert all the time. Renias must have told me a hundred times that tracking grizzlies was a bad idea.

We armed ourselves with a potent mustard-based spray that is used in the United States to ward off attacking bears and it provided us with a relative feeling of safety. Jim cautioned us as a canister of the spray had once gone off in his jeans pocket, nearly relieving him of his manhood! Strangely, that story seemed to give Renias some confidence as he saw how animated Jim was telling the story and obviously decided the spray was strong enough! In terms of danger, tracking grizzlies is a few clicks up from the black bears we'd tracked in Cuyama but we were more proficient at tracking bears this time around and had a lot of fun with our students.

On the fundraising front, however, our proposal wasn't yielding much, even though I thought the PowerPoint presentation I had created would be irresistible to any well-meaning philanthropist. Filled with lots of pretty pictures of Renias and me on foot with animals and various graphs and facts showing the decline in traditional skills of tracking in Africa, it did little to entice potential donors. After presenting in New York and San Francisco, no one seemed vaguely interested or prepared to commit any money; people only wanted to hear our thrilling stories of encountering lions and leopards on foot.

We left feeling despondent and perplexed as to why no one was moved to invest in our idea. Surely the demise of an ancient social environmental skill affects us all, I thought to myself, as tracking isn't only about walking in the bush in search of charismatic animals. The interwoven themes of tracking, animal conservation and African culture are all vital for the future sustainability of wilderness and wildlife. This is the message I was trying to convey to the Americans but I clearly wasn't getting it across.

The alarming disappearance of traditional tracking skills over the last four to five decades is an indictment on the conservation industry as a whole. As a historically African skill, wildlife tracking represents a direct means of engaging the land's custodians and those living in neighbouring communities close to game reserves, in the restoration of wilderness. But there is no incentive for the local people to protect something when there is little or no benefit accruing from the wildlife-based business activities in the vicinity. In many places, game reserves are viewed purely as elite enclaves, playgrounds for those wealthy enough to enjoy them. The preservation of wilderness areas should be inextricably linked to direct and meaningful participation by those villagers who often have no option but to stare through the wires of the high fences every day. Just like Jon had done as a little boy growing up.

Renias maintains that the animals in game reserves are merely seen as food by the majority of people, and if this is indeed true, then community participation and, particularly, environmental education should be a priority. I believe this should be a mandatory school subject for every child living in Africa, and is probably the only way communities will change how they see game reserves and what they represent.

The ecotourism and photographic safari industries have proven that animals are far more valuable when they are alive. The opportunities offered by the economy of wildlife for the neighbouring communities needs no selling, but it requires greater participation by its stakeholders to scale it up tenfold. Africa's unique selling point is its wildlife and our ability to deliver world-class safaris for visitors. Corridors need to be created and mega-parks developed, both of which will restore ancient animal movements and generate material benefit for local people.

The almost 8 billion people on Earth, combined with our domestic livestock, represent over 96 per cent of all mammals and we are literally eating away the last remnants of wildlife populations. The Earth has already lost 80 per cent of all wild animals, resulting in local extinctions and a concomitant loss of biodiversity that renders the system vulnerable; such is the impact humanity has had on nature.

THE REALISATION OF A DREAM

Conservation is more about changing people's hearts and minds than the animals because without the purposeful participation of the ever-increasing human population, we will almost certainly experience the complete demise of wild animals and wilderness areas. The situation is like a pressure cooker and if conservationists hope to make gains for wildlife, we all need to change our focus. If we can create safe havens for animals, they will thrive; if we take away their space, they disappear. It's as simple as that and it is underpinned by a secure, mutually beneficial relationship between the people, the animals and the landscape.

The tracker mentality resides deep in the DNA of most, if not all, human beings. In the ecotourism industry, the trackers find the animals for the discerning paying travellers and, along with their knowledge of animal behaviour, they provide the first line of safety on a safari. From a conservation management perspective, wildlife tracking is a skill necessary for efficient anti-poaching operations. Wildlife protection teams need trackers to find alleged poachers on the run or to track wounded animals, but there is a stark lack of experienced trackers among many of the anti-poaching units in southern Africa. The parks desperately need the services of expert trackers to counter the growing incursion rate by poaching gangs, who are in many instances, masters of the bush.

Although it is an ancient, and some say outdated, skill, Renias and my agenda has always been, and continues to be, to demonstrate that tracking has relevance in modern conservation efforts. We needed someone to take us seriously in order to make this a reality.

Back in South Africa, deflated and demotivated, Renias and I considered returning to our day jobs at Londolozi as we had expended almost all of our money and effort with nothing to show for it. But things often fall into place when you are least expecting it. I met a woman by the name of Gaynor Rupert. Gaynor is the daughter-in-law of the well-known South African entrepreneur, the late Dr Anton Rupert. I knew of the Rupert family and their support of conservation through the Rupert Nature Foundation and the Peace Parks Foundation (PPF) that Dr Rupert, together with Nelson Mandela and HRH Prince Bernhard of the Netherlands, co-founded in 1997. PPF was established to facilitate the formation of transfrontier conservation areas in southern Africa and over the last two decades has knitted together several transboundary-protected areas spanning 1 million square kilometres of conservation land, a diplomatic triumph for wildlife.

Gaynor had heard about our work from a mutual friend by the name of Simon Morgan, and invited us to conduct a small-mammal survey of her family's farm in the Eastern Cape Karoo region, using tracking as the means of data collection. We gathered information on a variety of small animals resident in the area and the records ultimately formed the basis of an in-house fieldguide enjoyed by family and friends visiting the farm.

Renias and I completed that project and continued our quest of looking for sponsors for our tracking scheme. In order to earn some money, I did some work with Mike Boon, the founder of a pioneering company called Vulindlela, facilitating better relations between black and white employees in corporate South Africa. I also started evaluating the skills of trackers at various private game reserves, which was work that inspired me when I saw the trackers' responses to having their skills properly recognised.

In 2009, several months after we'd completed the work on the Rupert farm, I received a call from Gaynor. She must have seen what we were capable of and told me that she wanted to start a tracker training school, with Renias and me to be involved. Her call was like manna from heaven as we had all but given up on the idea, and I immediately called Renias to share the news with him.

We got going straight away. The first step was to find a suitable venue for the school. We needed a game reserve where we could conduct the training so we started to make enquiries with many of the reserves we had relationships with. While evaluating trackers at Samara Private Game Reserve near Graaff-Reinet the year before, Renias and I had met the owner, Sarah Tompkins, who we had immediately formed a rapport with. Fifteen years earlier, Sarah and her husband Mark had assembled eleven ecologically bankrupt sheep farms to restore a thriving Karoo sanctuary teeming with local indigenous animals and had created Samara.

It is a perfect tracking venue and Sarah was immediately receptive to our idea of housing the Tracker Academy on her land. She offered us a building to accommodate our students and the land we could operate from, with no costs involved other than our utilities. Sarah was fiercely supportive of us right from the start and was also instrumental in securing our first trainer at Samara, master tracker Karel 'Pokkie' Benadie. Pokkie had worked at the Karoo National Park for some 34 years and was certified as a master tracker. He is a Karoo specialist with exceptional knowledge not only of animal tracking, but of small plants and their medicinal value, and he was going to be in charge of our Karoo operation.

Using tracking as the means to collect data, Pokkie was pivotal in unearthing the seasonal feeding habits of black rhino in the Karoo and his findings were eventually published in a well-known scientific journal. Pokkie brought his wife, Janetta, who started out as the camp attendant but quickly became the academy's operations manager.

Renias and I then spoke to our long-standing friend Dave Varty, who was equally supportive of the project and its mission. He agreed to provide us with the space to open the second base of the school at Londolozi and constructed a purpose-built facility for our tracker students. We now had two ecologically diverse training bases, both exceptional venues for teaching tracking. It was important that we had game reserves that offered good densities of animals and substrate that was conducive to successful tracking, and in Samara and Londolozi we had both.

On 5 January 2010, Gaynor Rupert founded and funded the Tracker Academy. It was a day I had always dreamed about and it had finally become a reality. We chose the hyaena, the best tracker in the animal kingdom, as our logo. Hyaenas are extraordinary caretakers of the next generation and this quality is something that we as humans share with them; it is also a tenet vital to restoring ancient tracking skills. Plus, hyaenas had always been my favourite animal and it made me think of when I was a boy and spent all those nights at my Uncle Skattie's farm. Pokkie and Renias were our hyaenas-in-chief, the head trainers who would teach the next generation. I took on the positions of general manager, part-trainer and co-assessor, a relatively broad role that was needed in the early stages of our untested project.

Tracker Academy was officially 'born' when we accepted our first group of eight students, representing almost every province of the country. The academy became a training division of the SA College for Tourism (SACT), which is chaired by Gaynor and operates under the auspices of the PPF. The SACT also trains 90 disadvantaged women every year on a sponsored hospitality skills programme, many of whom are deployed in jobs throughout the PPF's transfrontier conservation areas.

It was a perfect fit for Tracker Academy and to be associated with such legitimate conservation organisations is an ongoing honour. The bold and visionary action taken by Gaynor brought our long-standing dream to establish a formal tracker training school to fruition. But it also set in motion the basis for enabling the unrecognised to be officially acknowledged – for the rare and unique skillset of tracking to hopefully make a positive impact on the relationship between the game reserves and their local custodians, notwithstanding the development of skills.

For the first time in South Africa, people living in poor rural areas adjacent to wildlife reserves and national parks, many without any opportunities, had the chance to be trained as professional wildlife trackers for the conservation industry, in order to earn a decent living.

We decided to make the programme twelve months long, with

the students stationed at Samara for the first six months and at Londolozi for the second six months. Pokkie and Renias bring a combined 70 years of practical wildlife experience, not to mention their exceptional technical ability, patience, and most importantly, the capacity to teach. The diversity of the two training biomes has proven to be a successful recipe for the curriculum. Students are immersed in two vastly different habitat types, affording them a fantastically comprehensive view of South African wildlife and tracking conditions.

Samara is essentially a semi-desert biome while Londolozi is bushveld. The programme delivers theoretical and practical components of tracking skills and we were forced to develop much of the training methodology from scratch, as no other permanent training facility was in operation at the time. Tracker Academy training prgramme was formally accredited in 2012 by CATHSSETA, one of the training authorities that oversees skills development in South Africa. It is also the first and only specialist tracker training school in the world that trains professional trackers over a full-time, formally accredited course. We received formal endorsement from FGASA, the important, industry-recognised body we are aligned with, essential in upholding the credibility of the certificates we issue.

Being aligned with these two bodies gives the programme academic integrity and genuine credibility and is overall a great victory for the traditional skills of tracking. A few years after opening, the academy was a finalist in the international Tourism for Tomorrow Peoples Award, held in China, for our work with rural communities in conservation.

Renias was adamant from the start that our graduates had to find employment if the Tracker Academy was to be successful. There was no use training trackers just because *we* liked tracking. We needed to deploy our graduates to permanent jobs where they could demonstrate their practical skills and prove their intrinsic value to wildlife conservation. Renias always says that our students must be able to consistently track and find animals such as lions and leopards for the companies they're employed at, and so the trailing component of the programme quickly became the main focus.

Private game reserves and national parks will not employ 'hood ornaments', a derogatory term given to those so-called trackers who simply sit on the front of the vehicle and point out the obvious. It is vital that our graduates are able to be deployed anywhere and immediately prove their ability to understand and monitor wildlife densities, and then begin to track and find animals for whatever outcome is requested of them.

Although we enjoyed endorsements and accreditations, the practical outcomes needed to be clear and evident, otherwise we risked losing credibility in the industry and, indeed, our formal recognition as a tracker school.

A few years after we opened, a tracking organisation in existence prior to Tracker Academy had been hard at work trying to undermine the academy's work. They had attempted to de-accredit our training programme and after unsuccessful attempts to convince the training authority to do so, they turned to FGASA and put pressure on them to either cancel or control our endorsement via their organisation. We were accused of weakening the standards of tracking in the country and that we were operating in isolation.

We *were* operating in isolation since we were the only organisation actually training trackers on full-time accredited programmes; others were only testing trackers. I was advised by a number of people that I would do well submitting to this organisation. People determined to destabilise our work and aligned with this organisation then started circulating rumours that Renias and I were getting rich on Tracker Academy. How I wish that had been true!

There was a relentless effort by a small group of people to discredit the academy within the industry, a tiny industry by global standards. Our credibility and quality of training and assessing were being severely misrepresented. I even considered capitulating and surrendering to this organisation due to the pressure that was being placed on us.

I was focused on developing tracking skills for professional practitioners in South Africa for the benefit of conservation and I disliked the fact that a small elite group of poorly representative people, in terms of racial diversity, were vying to control its administration. My view was that future trackers should be able to decide for themselves which tracking school to enrol at or what assessment to take, in the same way school-leavers are free to decide which university to attend.

Even so, I started to doubt everything we had done and was deeply unsettled by the comments that were circulating. Finally, I asked Boyd to tell me what he thought. 'Perhaps they're right,' I said to him, 'maybe we should close down and get back in line.' His response changed everything for me. In the most matter-of-fact tone he simply said, 'Your excellence is hurting them.' I had never felt so emotionally invested in something as I had over those past three or four months, and the thought of what could have happened to the academy completely consumed me. Boyd's words put everything into perspective and I knew I had to fight back.

My determination and belief in the academy were never more tested than when, a few months later, we were judged by FGASA on the annual verification visit. This is a visit that all endorsed training providers are required to undergo and it is in place to ensure trainers and assessors meet the required industry standards. The verification process is carried out in much the same way as a school inspector assesses standards at a school.

We were accustomed to these visits and enjoyed demonstrating the quality of our training and assessments. But on this particular occasion, days before the scheduled visit, instead of only the standards director from FGASA judging us, I was informed that a delegation of five people, comprising members of the other tracking organisation and a few FGASA representatives, would be coming to inspect us. Like a kudu that has just sensed a leopard, I was on full alert and became concerned we were being set up to fail in front of FGASA. I was immediately suspicious that there was an alternate agenda at play and the red flag was why five people were needed to carry out the inspection. From a logistical point of view, this was an issue as Londolozi didn't have enough space to accommodate everyone so alternative accommodation had to be arranged elsewhere in the reserve.

On day one of the visit, we met the delegation at the junction of two main roads in the northern part of Londolozi's land. We were to conduct our assessment of the students' knowledge of identifying and interpreting animals' tracks and signs for the delegation to examine. I imagined what it must have been like for our schoolteachers when the provincial inspector arrived in their classes as my heart rate went up and stayed there for most of the day. I felt our every move was being closely scrutinised and I was unnerved by an undertone of officious passive-aggressive behaviour from some of the inspectors. It became clear from the outset that this verification visit was going to be different from ones we had had in the past.

I cautiously observed as our students performed their craft, while the judgemental energy seemed to descend like a thick mist. Layers of tension developed over the poor students and over us as their teachers, and the unspoken agenda of some of the inspectors was very clear. I felt for the welfare of our students and the pressure they were feeling, but at the same time I knew we couldn't afford for anyone to fail the assessment.

The inspectors, some of South Africa's best trackers, meticulously checked every question and answer. It was the students' penultimate assessment of the year and it meant passing or failing the year-long programme. The assessment had the potential to end the academy too. Undeterred by the presence of all the apparently 'superior' trackers, the students decoded track after track like professionals, and I sensed their confidence grow as the day unfolded.

Noting how accurately they were answering the questions, Renias and I started to ask more and more complex questions in a risky but highly rewarding attempt to prove the academy's excellence. In the end, after what was in many ways an unfair assessment, considering the unnecessary and excessive pressure brought to bear on the young men by the inspectors, the students all passed the assessment with scores of 85 per cent and above. A student by the name of Ivan Buregoo achieved 100 per cent.

The following day, Ivan successfully tracked a pride of lions, unassisted, for hours in the hot sun to again prove and reinforce the standards of Tracker Academy. In difficult and often stony terrain, he stuck to the trail like a bloodhound on a fox scent and demonstrated the result of thousands of hours of painstaking and thorough training. Ivan was the sucker punch we needed.

Despite this victory, the inspectors were unremitting and began interviewing the students one-on-one, out of sight and out of earshot. I was intrigued as to what some of the inspectors were asking and following the pedantic prying of our assessment techniques, they then asked why the circles Renias and I drew around the track questions were of a specific size! 'Your circles are too small, why?' one quizzed.

Are they being serious? I thought. I realised they were trying to rile me and so what started out as robust, reasonably constructive debates, rapidly disintegrated into a cold-war atmosphere and ultimately into full-blown direct conventional conflict with shouting matches laced with profanity. In the penultimate feedback meeting, Ian Thomas, our long-time mentor who I'd asked at the last minute to join the assessment and support us, and who was usually a calm man, was breathing fire!

On the last evening of the verification visit, I took the inspectors back to the camp they were staying at north of Londolozi and while I was driving, I heard the sound of my own voice quietly emanating from the pocket of the person sitting directly behind me. The next day, while we were in the last meeting with the inspectors and the FGASA representatives, I challenged the person directly as to whether she had been recording all the debates and altercations over the duration of their visit. She initially denied it but I decided to push my point as I was certain of what I had heard and she finally owned up and admitted she had been recording us. The FGASA chairman, Vernon Cresswell, who was in attendance, was visibly shocked by such unprofessional behaviour by one of his senior executives. He called off the entire verification visit and straight away apologised for the unauthorised and unethical recording of our meetings. The ulterior motive of the visit was clear and, like a boil being lanced, everything came out, and it was clear the FGASA standards director had no knowledge of the other inspectors' intentions.

Renias sauntered up to me as everyone was leaving and cheekily said, 'Buti, well done. You heard the alarm call this time!' Had I not heard the sound of my voice coming from that recorder, we might have fought a long, hard battle to have the academy formally recognised by the industry in South Africa. A few weeks later, Tracker Academy was given unequivocal endorsement as a specialist tracker training school, and we've enjoyed a great relationship with FGASA, under standards director Brian Serrao and chairman Vernon Cresswell, ever since.

Looking back, I can see how Tracker Academy effectively disrupted the wildlife tracking industry by offering full-time training services, as well as an alternative option for qualifying as a tracker. In the midst of the tension we nearly capitulated but the successes we've enjoyed in the past ten years, with excellent student results and the high deployment rate of our graduates in permanent conservation jobs, has made it a particularly fulfilling experience. I learnt that backing down is not an option if you're sure in your heart that your venture is honest and genuinely adds value to its beneficiaries, whether through a commercial or not-for-profit entity.

Gaynor's decision to establish Tracker Academy in the first place and her graciousness, wisdom and continued support has produced more than 170 formally accredited professional trackers for the ecotourism, anti-poaching and animal-monitoring sectors of the conservation industry, of which 90 per cent have found permanent jobs. Many of them send me photos of houses they've built, cars they've bought and the families they are raising – all acquired through offering the services of ancient tracking skills.

We recently added a third training campus at Tswalu Kalahari Reserve to focus on the training needs of trackers in the Northern Cape, Namibia and Botswana, and now train a total of 24 students every year. Our ongoing vision for Tracker Academy is to create more campuses around the world, wherever indigenous tracking skills are historically prevalent and wherever they can be used as a relevant and valuable tool in conservation management, wildlife protection and ecotourism.

Calming elusive predators

With our tracker graduates slowly being employed in the conservation industry over the last decade, the Tracker Academy began to receive praise for their trailing skills. We've always put great emphasis on the trailing element as it's the rarest component of the tracking skillset that takes the longest to learn. Before you can trail you must first be able to identify and interpret animal sign. This identification process represents the reading of individual animals' traffic, like the letters of the alphabet, whereas following an animal's trail is the recognition of patterns that leads to the comprehension of the animal's activity; comparable to reading a language.

The academy is always looking for ways to demonstrate the high standards of trailing that we instil in our students. We got a great opportunity to do this a few years ago, when Pokkie and two of our top graduates were asked to track and find a young male lion that had broken out of the Karoo National Park near Beaufort West. The park's officials, police and tracking dogs had tried for three days to find the lion fugitive but were unsuccessful. On the fourth day, Pokkie and his charges were transported to the last known position of the lion, and dropped approximately 5 kilometres west of the park.

After three days of constant tracking, through some of the most rugged and challenging terrain, Pokkie and his two students found the lion feeding on a kudu carcass some 20 kilometres west of the park. The story went viral and I fielded many phone calls from television channels as far afield as the United States. The CEO of a large South African retailer was so impressed that he was moved to donate free food supplies to Tracker Academy for a year.

The tracking and habituation of elusive predators is an area we unknowingly created the need for and we are now actively preparing our graduates to fulfil this role. Using the techniques developed at Londolozi in the 1970s and 1980s, Renias spends much time equipping our students with the skills necessary to find and slowly form a relationship with shy predators. Again, there was no blueprint to follow and we have had to develop the theoretical material and training methods ourselves.

The depth and quality of the academy's training was put to the ultimate test when we were invited to track and habituate jaguars in the Pantanal region of Brazil, home to the world's biggest wetland. Mario Haberfeld, a well-known Brazilian racing-car driver turned conservationist, had visited Londolozi to experience South African ecotourism first-hand. He was excited after accompanying Renias and me on a training session to pursue the trail of a lion one early morning as he had recently started a jaguar habituation project on a large swathe of land in a private reserve called the Caiman Ecological Refuge in the south-western state of Mato Grosso do Sul in Brazil.

Although a healthy population of jaguars inhabited the area, very few guests visiting the two luxury lodges on Caiman actually saw them. Mario wanted to change this and his mission was to foster environmental conservation and socioeconomic development of the Pantanal region using the enigma of the jaguar as the catalyst. After witnessing the practical tracking skills required to successfully follow and find wild animals in a large wilderness area, Mario immediately invited us to Caiman to ascertain whether the same could be achieved with jaguars in one of the world's largest wetlands.

We flew to Sao Paulo and after a connecting flight to Campo Grande, drove to Caiman, arriving there at 3am, not knowing quite where we'd ended up. The Pantanal region is similar in structure to the Okavango Delta, with grassy openings interspersed with islands of dense woodland that is perfect jaguar country. What we didn't realise is that those same thickets were also perfect for trillions of mosquitoes; at times we struggled to even see the tracks properly through the haze! The soil is sandy and holds the tracks well, which is good for tracking, but the vegetation is exceptionally thick in places and there were areas where we had to chop our way through the undergrowth – resulting in us completely abandoning the cardinal rule of maintaining silence while tracking a large predator.

It is a beautiful landscape but it's hot, humid and uncomfortable.

On the second day, Renias and I tracked a single male jaguar for a few hours until we heard it jump into the water ahead of us. Even though we'd located the animal, we didn't even get a glimpse of it, giving us the sense that jaguars were obviously very nervous of people. We learnt that jaguars love water and their preferred prey is the caiman, similar to the Nile crocodile, among a long list that includes peccaries, snakes, monkeys, deer, tapirs, frogs and fish. I found it fascinating to learn that jaguars will stalk and kill caimans with a fierce bite to the back of the head, and we were told they will even swim through deep water to ambush a caiman basking in the sun on an island in the river.

The ever-present bodies of water posed a constant challenge to our tracking efforts and meant we often had to leave the tracks, find a way around the water and then start following again. A local cowboy told us that the caimans pose little threat to humans. 'You can walk in the water, guys,' encouraged one of them; information Renias and I chose to ignore. Some years before, I'd been involved in helping Boyd survive a crocodile attack at Londolozi and had seen what a crocodile can do with just one bite, so we were not going to test the caimans' friendliness in their territory. Even if that meant we took longer to track the jaguars, we were happy to avoid wading through caiman-infested waters!

In ten days of tracking at Caiman, we established that you could effectively track and find jaguars using the same methods of tracking lions in Africa, meaning it would be possible to deploy some of our graduates to carry out the project. Although there are differences in the fauna and flora, the universal principles of tracking still apply.

A month later, we deployed two of our top tracker graduates, Andrea Mathebula and Richard Mthabine, who hail from rural villages in Mpumalanga and Limpopo respectively, to Caiman to track the jaguars with the aim of learning about their movements and ultimately to form a relationship with them for the benefit of Caiman's tourism operations. Richard and Andrea's mission was to build a trusting relationship with the jaguars that enabled the guests visiting Caiman to view them in their natural habitat. If we were successful it would be a great coup for the reserve and lodges in the area.

A habituated predator is a learnt behaviour by the animal and while the animal retains all its natural instincts and behaviour, it grows accustomed to the tourism activities. The leopards at Londolozi, for example, have learnt that people sitting in an open-top, dark-green-coloured Land Rover pose no threat to them, nor do they represent a source of food. But habituated predators are very specific and if the three rows of seats are removed from a game drive vehicle, or the vehicle is a different colour, the cat immediately becomes hyper vigilant and untrusting. They won't allow the unusually shaped or different-coloured Land Rover to approach them and will constantly stare or snarl at the vehicle in warning, essentially telling you to keep your distance.

This became evident when there was an animal disease outbreak in the southern Kruger Park, and I had to travel with the veterinarian in his white bakkie to dart a sick lion. Because the vehicle was white and looked different from the Land Rovers we used on the game drives, the ones the lions were used to seeing, it managed to evade us and we struggled to get close enough to shoot a dart. Habituated predators learn very quickly what is out of place and will react accordingly if the human element changes in any way. That said, they maintain their natural behaviour irrespective of whether they are habituated or not. If a leopard or jaguar is found on foot, it will still move away or demonstrate aggression like any wild animal would respond under those circumstances.

Mhangene's relaxed demeanour around Renias and me had less to do with how habituated she was but more to do with her uniquely calm character. We have come to realise that predators possess strong individual character traits that need to be respected, as some are more aggressive or timid than others. But in all instances, their instinctual fear of humans remains intact, despite being accustomed to humans, and a habituated leopard will still hunt, kill, reproduce and interact with other species naturally. In all the habituation projects that we've been involved with at the academy, as well as Londolozi's well-documented 40-year relationship with habituated leopards, not a single animal has been lost to poaching or any kind of human persecution.

If we could achieve the successful habituation of the jaguars in Caiman, it would be of tremendous benefit to the tourism operation and the future preservation of the species in the Pantanal. Like so many places around the world, Brazilian farmers have waged war against the local predators in an effort to protect their livestock. With the growing beef industry in Brazil, the jaguars may have little hope of surviving. Mario's project, Associação Onçafari, aims to prove that the economy of wildlife, through ecotourism, is a viable alternative to consumptive cattle farming, the idea being that humans and animals can partner for the benefit of all.

Andrea and Richard had not travelled to any major cities

before, let alone flown halfway around the world to a foreign country to track an unknown predator. In my first Skype call to check in, they told me that tracking the jaguars 'was good' but they were struggling with the food saying, 'today we ate rice and beans and tomorrow will be beans and rice!' In spite of having to get accustomed to life in Brazil, they performed exceptionally well and managed to locate several different jaguars on numerous occasions; their efforts contributed to a dramatic increase in jaguar sightings on Caiman. They also trained a local Brazilian man while tracking the jaguars, giving the project long-term sustainability. On one particular day, they managed to successfully track and find a mating pair of jaguars that a friend of mine, Adam Bannister, who was helping with the project, was able to capture on film.

Four years after Andrea and Richard's project with the jaguars, Mario reported that more than 700 jaguar sightings had been recorded by guests visiting the lodges in Caiman in that year alone. This was an astounding outcome and triumph for ancient tracking skills and ecotourism. In Gaynor Rupert's words, the project in Brazil is 'an example of South Africa exporting skills for the benefit of international conservation'. Andrea and Richard's extreme patience, refined tracking skills and constant respect for the jaguars they pursued are the key factors that made that project a success.

Since that inaugural project in Brazil, we have conducted successful habituation projects in countries such as Rwanda and Botswana. At Wilderness Safaris's Magashi lodge in Rwanda, trackers started the habituation project there six months prior to the construction of the lodge and their efforts were rewarded when the first guests saw a leopard.

In 2019, at a Relais & Châteaux meeting, Shan and Dave Varty mentioned Tracker Academy's work to the director of Awasi, a prominent hotel company operating high-end ecotourism operations in Argentina and Chile. The Awasi concession in the region of Magallanes in southern Chile boasts a good mountain lion population but due to constant pressure and persecution by local sheep farmers, the already secretive mountain lions have turned into elusive animals that only the luckiest guests get a glimpse of.

In August 1995, in the area of the Awasi concession, nature struck and delivered over a metre of snow, killing some 170 000 sheep and over 10 000 cattle. This heavily curtailed the livestock ranching and in many instances put local farmers out of business. Some farmers simply did not have the capital to restock their farms with sheep and cattle and were forced to leave their lands vacant. With fewer ranchers and gauchos shooting the mountain lions that had been previously competing for space with their livestock, the population started to recover, to the extent that some farmers started running tours from the local town and took people to see and photograph the cats.

Dave suggested that Tracker Academy assist Awasi with habituating the mountain lions, and before long Renias and I were en route to Chile to establish whether a project to habituate mountain lions in some of the world's most inhospitable wilderness, Patagonia, was even possible. Before we left, I showed Renias a few photos of Patagonia and explained that most of the landscape comprises rock, making the project a fairly difficult one. Unfazed, he simply said, 'Buti, let's go, we will work it out.'

I considered for a moment that Renias's love of travel might have been clouding his judgement! I was concerned that the substrate might not hold a track and that we were attempting the impossible. The more imagery and videos I looked at, the less convinced I was that we would be able to successfully track and find a mountain lion in the vast rocky area. Dave, by contrast, had great confidence in our ability.

As with each project, Renias and I usually conduct an initial *in situ* due diligence to see whether the use of practical tracking skills to habituate the specific predator is even feasible. We design the project by establishing the areas most conducive to tracking success, good tracking terrain with impressionable soil, high predator density and accessibility to tourism activities, and where these elements overlap forms our target area. There's no use in tracking, finding and forming a relationship with an animal that you cannot get to, and the overlap and combination of these factors give the best chance of success.

We've also learnt that it's important to identify the individual predators with calm personalities. Sometimes, because of a bad experience with humans or like the angry Tugwaan, no amount of habituation effort will necessarily work to settle some predators. When working with habituating leopards, we usually focus on the females and mothers with cubs, as they move in considerably smaller territories than the males. One of the reasons Richard and Andrea were so successful with the jaguars is because they chose their targets well and did not waste time tracking those they deemed as 'bayiza', a Shangaan slang word for 'silly'.

Renias and I stepped off the aircraft in Punta Arenas, the capital city of the area near the tip of Chile's southernmost Patagonia region, into a bracing 1°C. As I got to the top of the stairs to disembark the aeroplane, a baggage handler offered, 'Welcome to warm day in Punta Arenas!' and Renias stared at him disbelievingly, already shivering in his flimsy fleece. Once we got onto the tarmac, Renias walked to the edge of the runway and, tapping his foot on the frozen stony ground, he turned and looked at me quizzically.

'Well, now there's no turning back, Buti,' I responded as I hurried for the warmth of the terminal building.

'Buti, this is going to be like tracking in my freezer!' Renias responded incredulously.

Punta Arenas is situated on the Strait of Magellan connecting the Atlantic and Pacific oceans and is often used as a base for excursions to Antarctica. We left Punta Arenas and drove northwards for four hours, circumnavigating the snow-capped mountains to the west and eventually arrived in a small town called Puerto Natales. Aside from Puerto Natales being the gateway to the Torres del Paine National Park and Awasi the neighbouring reserve, the town is also the port for boats touring the Patagonian fjords. Utterly exhausted after a gruelling 32-hour journey from Londolozi, we collapsed into our beds in our tiny, but most importantly heated, prefabricated accommodation that night.

The following morning, our host Cristian Asun Miller, Awasi's head guide, arrived with the most welcome gift – thermal clothing that could withstand the extreme Patagonian climate. My weather app showed that the anticipated high temperature for that day was going to be minus 1°C so the thermal clothes were crucial if we were going to track outside! When I showed Renias what we needed to wear, he just said, 'Haikona,' while shaking his head. And he proceeded to take a photo of me in the black thermals telling me I looked like a Navy Seal!

Donned in our finest, we drove out the camp in a westerly direction with a magnificent view of the early-morning golden sunrays shining onto the three signature towers of the Torres del Paine mountains. They are located inside the Torres del Paine National Park, a wilderness of 227 000 hectares in extent. Cristian told us that we should be proud to be South African because a team of South African mountaineers in the 1970s were the first climbers to make a free ascent of the east face of the completely vertical, 2 800-metre high, Central Tower also known as the 'Central Tower of Paine'. This was a mountaineering feat that many of the local Chilean people deemed a death wish.

As we drove, we noticed a few vulture-like large birds called condors sitting on the ground ahead in the distance. Their presence, together with that of birds called caracara of the falcon family, was a possible indication of a fresh carcass nearby. Primarily a scavenger like our African vultures, the Andean condor is considered the largest flying land bird in the world, when combining its weight and wingspan, and it has incredible longevity, reaching up to 70 years of age in some cases. Cristian told us that the mountain lions avoid areas where condors are regularly active because the birds are such voracious feeders. From the exceptionally large size of the bird, they could present a real challenge to many other predators, especially if they congregate in flocks.

We stopped the vehicle and went to investigate what the condors were feeding on and this took us down a relatively steep slope in the direction of the national park. Our guide, Cristobal Sanchez, looked through his binoculars and said there was a dead sheep and that it was probably killed by a mountain lion. I scanned the landscape with my binoculars and was struck by the similarity of the vegetation to the Karoo, the only exception being that Patagonia has more snow-capped mountains and lakes. We walked up to the sheep's carcass and saw bits of wool scattered around the kill on the stubby black shrubs that are common to the area.

Renias and I immediately began searching for tracks, hoping to find one of a mountain lion but the ground was still frozen solid, as was the spilled sheep's blood, even though it was already 10am. I had been excited at the prospect of finding and following a mountain lion's trail, but once we were on the ground it became blatantly clear that it was going to be a very challenging tracking proposition.

The bite marks on the sheep's neck and evidence of a predator feeding from between the hind legs were clear – it is a common portion of the carcass that carnivores start eating once they have killed their prey. The evidence clearly indicated that a large carnivore had killed, or had certainly fed on, that sheep. Even though the mountain lion had likely spent quite some time feeding at the site, we could not make out a single track. Cristobal wanted to keep walking because he felt he had a sense of where the mountain lion might have gone. I asked him to give us some time to explore the area but I think he probably had a dim view of what I'm sure he saw as complete inexperience on our part. The previous evening some of the guides had questioned Renias and I as to how we planned to track in such stony and difficult conditions and my answer was just that we were 'going to try'. Not a very encouraging response!

'Here's a track, Buti,' Renias said to me, after having scouted the immediate area around the sheep's carcass for a good few minutes. It was probably the faintest track I'd ever seen and I really had to use my imagination to try to see what Renias was seeing. I could make out two reasonably clear toe impressions but the rest of the track was exceedingly obscure. Cristobal also looked at the track and I waited for him to challenge us but he simply said, 'Good,' which made we wonder if he could even see the track.

That morning, Cristobal was supposed to be orientating us and showing us some of the areas where the Awasi guides believed the mountain lions were frequenting, but I asked him whether we could follow the track we had found instead. He was under instruction from his boss and I got the sense he didn't want to disobey him or veer too far off the plans for the day. Following the tracks meant we would be disrupting the plans for the day, but I knew we needed to take full advantage of the opportunity and being agile in our thought processes and developing optionality in our approach made us good trackers. And that day, in those tracking conditions, represented the chance we needed to take.

With a slight show of indignation, Cristobal agreed to follow us as we tracked the mountain lion. The tracks were not heading in the direction he'd predicted but I agreed with Renias, not only because of where the track was pointing, but I also surmised that as the mountain lions had been persecuted in that area, they would in all likelihood want to return to the safety of the national park during the day, after having killed a sheep in a place it must have known was dangerous.

We continued on our track and walked along a natural path in a westerly direction, down a slope towards a large river called Las Chinas, which forms the boundary with the national park. 'There will be a natural crossing point across the river that the mountain lions will use,' said Renias to Cristobal. Cristobal agreed and pointed directly ahead. Renias then looked back at me and smiled knowingly. 'I will find it, mfo,' he said. Further along the trail, I noticed a tiny piece of bloodied wool on the ground that I showed to Renias. He gave me a satisfied grin and agreed we were definitely in the right area as the wool must have dropped from the muzzle of the mountain lion after having fed on the sheep, or perhaps it stopped to preen and clean itself and the residual piece of wool had dropped on the ground. We couldn't be certain but the wool was clear evidence that we were still on the mountain lion's trail.

An icy wind started to blow, which launched an assault on my nose, ears and feet, and I had to stop every few metres and do a few star jumps to try to warm up. 'My nose is throbbing,' I stammered to Renias in Shangaan and he replied, 'Because it's too big, mfo. Mine is small that's why I'm fine,' demonstrating his sense of humour even under the toughest of conditions. We had never experienced temperatures that cold and it was beginning to take its toll on our energy levels. I had lost all feeling in my feet and hands, and I rued the fact that I hadn't purchased proper gear when we were in Punta Arenas, something Cristian had strongly suggested we do.

The 'cold weather' clothing we'd bought in South Africa turned out to be completely insufficient for the conditions we were experiencing. Fortunately, the thermal wear Cristian had given us kept our bodies reasonably warm, but our extremities were slowly beginning to freeze due to the body's response of redirecting blood to the core and vital organs. Parts of my body I didn't even know about were shivering and my speech was slightly slurred, something I was a bit concerned about.

I looked up at the three towers of Torres del Paine and immediately had renewed respect for mountaineers and for people who've taught themselves to endure the extreme cold. Cristobal must've seen me looking at the mountain and told me it was minus 15°C at its peak! He could see we were taking strain and kindly offered us each a chocolate bar that we devoured and then immediately asked for another.

A small group of guanacos, tawny coloured llama-like animals native to South America, were grazing on the slope below us and I considered that the mountain lion had probably moved beyond them as the animals appeared very relaxed. Guanacos occupy the same family as camels and can weigh up to 140 kilograms and I was astounded by their size, especially since there didn't appear to be too much lush vegetation for them to feed on. I recalled research I had come across that showed that mammals that live in colder climates are usually heftier than those that inhabit warmer climes, and heavier, bulkier animals have a smaller surface-area-to-volume ratio, helping reduce heat loss in freezing conditions. Cristobal also explained that guanacos make a high-pitched bleating alarm call if they detect a mountain lion. 'We use the guanacos a lot to help us find mountain lions,' he said with little excitement in his voice. I still think he was convinced that we were wasting his time following imaginary mountain lion tracks.

We proceeded for another fifteen minutes and Renias then spotted another equally faint track on the ground. I started to feel excited that we were close to finding the mountain lion. Renias always displays a subtle change in his body language, which I don't think he's even aware of, when he thinks we are close to finding an animal we're tracking. He starts to move a little quicker, he speaks faster, he looks up more often and there's generally a positive energy about him. Whether it was my own intuition or I was unconsciously reading Renias's energy, I felt we were close.

I looked back to where we had found the sheep's carcass and it was clear the mountain lion was heading back towards its place of refuge in the Torres del Paine National Park. The only question was how far we were behind it. In Africa, we can tell the age of a carcass by the state and colour of the flesh and the flies and associated smell, but because the sheep's flesh and blood was already frozen, we couldn't judge how old the kill was. But the mountain lion had eaten less than 20 per cent of the carcass, so we could deduce it had been killed very early that morning.

Eventually we got to a high point above the Las Chinas River and had a good view of the water channel below. Cristobal then told us that the crossing point he knew of was slightly further upstream, as Renias predicted, and that we should go and check it. As we were about to turn and find a route down to the water's edge, he noticed something moving along the opposite bank of the river. 'Mountain lion!' he exclaimed. Renias and I scrambled for our binoculars but my hands had lost some fine motor control from the cold so it took me a good minute or so to line up my binoculars with the animal. And indeed it was a mountain lion — a young male striding along the opposite riverbank totally unaware of our presence and doing exactly as it would have had we not been there. I never believed that we would even track a mountain lion in Chile let alone be successful in finding and seeing one and Renias turned to me, gave me a high-five and said, 'I told you, mfo!'

While walking back to the vehicle, and reflecting on the day's success, I decided tracking mountain lions would be an excellent project for our tracker graduates to tackle. The fact that the conditions were so challenging made it even better. As always, Renias was on my wavelength and he came up next to me and said, 'We must only send thinking trackers here. You won't be successful if you come here and think you will track like at Londolozi.' Yes, indeed ... thinking trackers.

Over the course of the next few days, Renias spotted a mother mountain lion and her four cubs high on a mountain edge. This particular family of mountain lions inhabits a territory located on a ranch, Estancia Laguna Amarga. The sheep were wiped out there by the snowfall of 1995 and the landowner allowed the natural wildlife to flourish after the disaster, in a mutually beneficial relationship where a thriving population of mountain lions is safe from persecution and the landowners earn an income from tourists coming to see the cats. With years of exposure to people on foot, the mountain lions on Estancia Laguna Amarga are like the leopards at

Londolozi – habituated but still wild.

We spent hours with that mother mountain lion and her cubs and slowly but surely they grew accustomed to our presence on foot. Eventually they were no more than 60 metres from us and although we got the odd growl from one of the youngsters, they were far less perturbed than I could possibly have imagined. In a remarkably short space of time these mountain lions had realised that we posed no threat to them.

With tourism growing in the area, more and more people are flocking to get a glimpse of the elusive and charismatic mountain lion. Sadly, not all of the ranchers in the area are as environmentally conscious as those at Awasi and Laguna Amarga, and many still shoot the mountain lions on sight for fear of them hunting and killing their sheep. This is an inevitable outcome as they are naturally occurring wild predators and it is an interaction that ultimately sets up a self-perpetuating cycle of human-wildlife conflict where no party really wins.

Renias and I met with a rancher by the name Jorge who told us he could see the benefits of partnering with the local wildlife through ecotourism, and he was ready to make the change after hundreds of years of his family farming on the land. He proudly explained that his first step in creating a relationship with the mountain lions was to keep his horses and cattle in open areas to avoid causing conflict – which he said 'is working well' to minimise the chances of mountain lions killing the foals and calves.

To demonstrate the success of the Londolozi model, Dave has invited those ranchers still intent on killing the mountain lions to visit Londolozi so they can witness the success of a mature example of a human-wildlife relationship. Renias extended this invitation to Jorge in order for him to witness, first-hand, the great potential of a thriving ecotourism business model. The area of Patagonia where Awasi, Estancia Laguna Amarga and Jorge's land are situated has the potential to become a world-class wildlife and tourist destination but the landowners, ranchers and shepherds need to agree on and internalise the concept of forming a relationship, a working partnership, with the wildlife in the area. There is a fine line between working against and with the local wildlife and, as I see it, the additional cost and effort to effectively protect the sheep can easily be offset by a profitable non-consumptive ecotourism operation. The trick is not to deny ranchers their beloved farming culture but instead to introduce mutually beneficial methods to improve livestock protection whilst simultaneously providing safe havens for wildlife.

Like at Caiman in the Pantanal, we have witnessed a gradual transition from intensive cattle ranching where the jaguars were the villains to a blended model that includes ecotourism, to ultimately a pure-bred economically viable ecotourism venture where the jaguars occupy centre stage.

Tracking racial prejudice

Renias and I have spent more than two decades together, working in close quarters, in varying conditions, for a variety of work outcomes. Each new venture we embarked upon or each destination we visited together brought unique challenges or reactions that needed to be overcome and reconciled. A long insular life in the bush predisposes you to a certain degree of parochialism and this means that travelling to new places requires a bit more planning.

Initially we routinely got sick after long flights, which made the ensuing work that much more challenging. Renias was used to his daily intake of pap and his stomach couldn't handle more than three days of Western food. We tried taking maize with us a few times but it often got confiscated at the airports.

The early days working together as a guide and tracker team were by far the simplest period and we experienced alignment on most issues. Our lives were straightforward and there was relatively little stress, with the exception of the odd fussy guest or a lean period of game viewing. But when we started travelling together to conduct presentations or tracking classes, we often slept in the same bed or tent or endured long-haul travel, sometimes for weeks on end, without our families. These trips took their toll, with Renias feeling homesick, and I grew weary of having to manage all the details of our travel and the courses we were presenting. Speaking Shangaan all the time was tiring for me as I needed to concentrate more than if I was speaking English, and Renias felt the same speaking a second language to people who struggled with his accent.

At Tracker Academy we have different styles of managing the students. Renias is not a disciplinarian and prefers to give people latitude whereas I don't allow much deviation from the accepted code of conduct. These differences sometimes cause friction between us, but the reason I believe our relationship has endured is because we were both prepared to acknowledge our differences and leverage each other's strengths.

We are a team just like any other, and we had to actively search for ways to find a compromise. We have done this with reasonable success, albeit far from perfect. Our diverse life circumstances have been a challenge but in order to succeed, we had to develop the same level of consistency in our interactions that married couples strive for.

Similarly, South Africans need to find harmony with each other and form the productive relationships that are possible between people of disparate ethnicities. Our country's victory in the 2019 Rugby World Cup was clear evidence of the potential that exists, but too often ingrained intolerance and bigotry from all races prevents us from becoming the world-beating country we've demonstrated we can be.

Instances of outright racism receive wide coverage in our national media but are a microcosm of the big picture and underlying issues. A Durban estate agent saying something disparaging about the African people on the beachfront, two Cape Town motorists fighting over a parking place and using abusive language towards one another, politicians stirring up racial disharmony and outrage or the former premier of the Western Cape making historically questionable and inappropriate remarks in the media are manifestations of a far greater crisis.

These outbreaks of malice fill me with disbelief and sadness as I have had the privilege of experiencing multiracialism from a positive and inclusive perspective in my time at Londolozi.

My family history goes back twelve generations as white South Africans. The family tree bears evidence of 301 years of history in this country. My great-great-grandfather, Daniel Petrus van den Heever, was affectionately known as 'Oom Daantjie', a miniaturisation despite the fact that he was seven feet tall! He was a member of the Cape Parliament who led the charge for the introduction of Dutch as the official language in South Africa, which in 1882 became Afrikaans.

Renias's family tree couldn't be more different than mine and a few years ago we decided to have our DNA tested. We discovered that our respective autosomal DNA connects us both to Sudan some 50 000 years ago. Renias's ancestors first migrated west through Nigeria, Cameroon and finally southwards towards southern Africa, while mine headed north into Eastern Europe, finally settling in the British Isles.

Different physical environments caused our ancestors to adapt physiologically to survive the conditions. Pale skin aids in the absorption of ultraviolet light, something that is in short supply in the northern latitudes, and lighter skin also assists with vitamin D synthesis. Darker pigmentation protects the skin against the harsh ultraviolet light produced by the bright African sun, a vital adaptation to surviving exposure on the sunny continent. Our anatomical differences are born of adaptive physiology and are superficial when compared with our much greater similarities.

Another commonality we share is the ancient hunter-gatherer lifestyle. Renias's ancestors thrived by hunting, gathering and trading and my DNA results revealed a 51 per cent genetic link to the hunter-gatherer haplogroup, meaning they were possibly inclined to that lifestyle and brought their hunting skills to Europe, where they took advantage of a warming trend occurring at the time on the European continent.

I have always been intrigued about my family heritage so about twenty years ago I travelled to the Karoo in search of my great-great-grandfather Oom Daantjie's only remaining grandson, Oom Koot van den Heever. He was in an old age home in Bethulie and was 96 years old. I entered his tiny room, greeted him and he looked up and squinted at me and said, 'Jy's nie 'n Van den Heever nie, jy's te kort ... 'n Van den Heever moet buig om hier in te kom.'

The feistiness and pride exhibited by that generation of Van den Heever men meant they wore their nationalist pride on their sleeves and derived their identity from their language, culture and the hardships they believed they endured. Many of these Afrikaner men deemed themselves culturally superior to other cultures and some even believed they were ordained by God. This belief system had its roots in Holland long before the settlers reached South Africa. Their dislike of 'uitlanders' was driven by their compulsive fear of losing their culture and religion and that it would be weakened by outside influences. When I walked into Oom Koot's room that day, there is no doubt my English accent, my physical appearance and most likely my body language, was 'different' enough for him to consider me an 'uitlander' and so his first reaction was to discriminate.

I left Oom Koot that day wondering to what extent I'd inherited some of these prejudiced beliefs from my forefathers. How much has my culture shaped my implicit bias? How much of my racial insecurity was nurtured in me by my external environment?

Social categorisation is common and mostly benign, that is until people start to form judgements that materially affect how we approach and interact with a member of another group. The classification of people, whether by race, gender, sexual orientation, or any other social construct, is a superficial attempt to make sense of the 'other' from a 'safe' distance. To me it is a sheltered excuse not to explore and appreciate an individual's unique life circumstance that happens to be dissimilar to your own.

When Renias and I first met, we were divided by language, culture and, of course, particular life experiences and, in many ways, we still are. I initially viewed Renias as someone who didn't trust white people and someone I couldn't trust either. I categorised him as a product of apartheid – uneducated and angry – while Renias saw me as another disinterested white guy, apprehensive to engage meaningfully with black people and a rich, young whitey who was temporary and exploitable. Renias told me once, 'To be honest, if I think about how we were treated by the apartheid government, I didn't trust white people because I could see they didn't care about us.'

The point is that we both held well-defined categorisations and opinions of each other that without putting in a lot of time and effort into would have foiled any chance of us forming a productive relationship.

The manifestation of gross intolerance between two groups of people is starkly evident by looking at the history of Rwanda. Renias and I were fortunate enough to visit the country when we travelled there to start a leopard habituation project in the Akagera National Park and then spent time in the capital city of Kigali. We specifically wanted to visit the genocide museum and, after viewing the mass graves, watching the shocking footage of the slaughter of people killing people, Renias and I stood in a darkened room and stared at the hundreds of crushed human skulls on display.

With his hand on his chin, Renias chillingly said, 'This could have been us, Buti,' referring to South Africa's peaceful yet tenuous transition to democracy in the same year as the Rwanda genocide.

Renias and I believe that South Africans need to actively and purposefully engage each other to fully reconcile so that we can move beyond the stubborn intolerance that remains in many of us – an ideal that is totally within our grasp and can be effected by ordinary people.

Renias and I regularly talk to companies that admit their struggles with diversity and prejudicial behaviour. The work arena and playing together in sports teams are two instances where people from an assortment of backgrounds are forced to interact closely and they are situations where we as South Africans have the opportunity to either build or destroy our unity. Following a lot of our presentations, we are never quite sure whether our message about the 'power of relationships' has been received and, more importantly, whether it has been internalised by the audience. Renias always tells people that they need to actually practise being more inclusive as it doesn't come naturally to humans. We have to be far more active in changing our mindset about other races if this country has any chance of healing, and we can't rely on the government to facilitate this process.

Employees who engage with one another on a daily basis, who actively learn about each other's cultures and face difficult situations together, create strong bonds, which have a myriad benefits for organisations. People from different cultures have unique ways of looking at the world, and bouncing ideas off one another often leads to innovations and resilient strategies. After spending a life working in and observing nature, it is abundantly clear to me that ecosystems with healthy biodiversity thrive. Diversity is fundamental to a flourishing natural system and, as partners in South Africa Inc., we should all see diversity as a gift and leverage it to our collective benefit.

Renias and my journey together has been a gradual untangling of biased thought; a dissolving of our respective prejudices so that we could see the essence of one another. With no shortcut available, it has taken a lot of time, loaded with experiences, failures and victories that are the building blocks of what is today an imperfect, yet reasonably productive, relationship between us.

Simply put, without one of us, none of the stories in this book would have happened. All relationships, especially multicultural ones, are a long-term investment whereby you slowly build shared trust and a sense of security with each other. I'm very aware that not everyone has twenty years to create a productive interracial relationship, but the demonstration of symbolic intent to engage with another human being is one way to start.

The simple act of holding my own forearm while shaking a black African person's hand nearly always results in a positive reaction from the recipient. The handshake conveys respect and trust and is a particularly virtuous way to begin an interaction.

I have noticed that both African and Afrikaans-speaking people prefer to begin interactions by engaging in humble banter, asking after their family and generally attempting to gain personal insights of the other person. The sometimes overly direct approach by Westerners can offend their African counterparts. By contrast, there is often misunderstanding when Westerners are labelled as racist or prejudiced for behaviour generated simply by their culture. There are so many acts significant to all the cultures in South Africa that we should recognise, learn and practise. A powerful first step to establishing a relationship with someone from another culture begins with an honest self-acknowledgement of your respective fears and biases about 'them'.

Over the years, by teaching me to speak Shangaan, Renias provided me with a tool that gave me access and a degree of insight into a culture that I wouldn't have been able to do without speaking the language. Similarly, I taught Renias to speak English so that he could understand me better. These were precious gifts we granted each other but they were also gifts we gave because we needed to improve and build on our relationship. Giving helped us with each other and within ourselves.

It was a long and sometimes tedious road as our early communications were often a mix of hand signals, speaking English and Afrikaans and, sometimes, out of sheer desperation, in much the same way it was developed on the mines, we used Fanagalo. Communication with Renias was one of my greatest frustrations and I desperately wanted to be able to have free-flowing dialogue with him but it seemed out of reach. I immediately became cognisant of the extent that language separated us and decided we needed to change that. Of course not everyone is a natural-born linguist, but it really is true that you are rewarded with bucket loads of appreciation simply for trying. The more Renias and I presented on the topic of intercultural cooperation and collaboration over the years, the more we realised its elusiveness in our audiences. Our mission has always been to raise awareness about our individual differences at work in an effort to highlight its benefits. At a certain point in the presentation, we ask people to raise their hands if they've ever spent the night at the home of a colleague from a culture different to theirs. In the almost ten years of us asking that question there's never been more than 5 per cent of an audience who have made that investment.

I naturally became sensitised to the subtle biases I noticed in conversations and the body language I witnessed, and my awareness of this made me start tracking people's conduct with the same verve that I trail leopards.

The aspect of cultural intolerance was emphasised when we arrived at a game lodge late one afternoon, after talking at a conference of a big audit firm in Johannesburg. We were at the lodge to evaluate a group of trackers and while sitting on the elevated deck of the lodge, I observed a group of black waiters and their white female camp manager busying themselves setting tables for dinner. The waiters chatted among themselves in Shangaan while the manager quietly plumped the cushions on the landing just above the veranda.

The camp manager, let's call her Holly, finished adjusting the cushions and then walked down the stairs towards the waiters. One of the waiters, I'll call him Thando, commented on Holly's evening dress and told her in Shangaan, 'You've dressed very beautifully tonight.' Holly responded quite abruptly, 'I don't understand you,' and so Thando repeated his compliment. 'I don't know what you're saying,' snapped Holly in a faintly irritable retort. It was fairly obvious and I have no doubt Thando also noticed her slight displeasure.

I had known Thando for a few years and I knew he was only partially literate, capable of taking breakfast orders. I had witnessed him on many occasions trying to teach the young white guides and camp staff how to speak Shangaan and I had always been struck by his generosity of spirit. He was a cheerful and extroverted man who enjoyed conversation.

Thando repeated the compliment but said it slower; I'm sure hoping Holly would understand him if he enunciated the words more clearly. Holly's response of 'What nonsense are you talking?' was said in a tone that was fairly serious in its accusation. I observed Thando carefully and saw him grimace briefly and then compose himself.

Thando was twice Holly's age and had worked at the game lodge for 25 years while Holly had only been there a few months. You could excuse her for not understanding the language, but it made me wonder whether Holly would have responded the way she did if Thando had been her white uncle. Probably not. Thando glanced quickly at his fellow waiters and then continued polishing the glasses on the table and said nothing further.

I decided to weigh in and I translated Thando's comment for Holly's benefit to which she replied, 'Oh ... thanks,' and smiled.

Why do white South Africans think it is acceptable to converse and interact with a black person in the way Holly did? Is it a youthful, generational thing or is it people's unconscious sense of superiority created to conceal feelings of guilt and non-belonging?

In Holly's case, she was fortunate that Thando was a forgiving person but if he hadn't been, she might have ruined her relationship with him before it even began. I have also witnessed unacceptable conduct from black people towards white people, but that is the point; it is our collective responsibility to improve the nature of our encounters by being a little more culturally aware of each other.

I'm sure if you ask Holly what happened that day with Thando she would in all likelihood say everything was fine between them. That is implicit bias. By contrast, Thando probably made an assumption, based on Holly's disrespect towards him, that white people are mean and audacious, when in reality Holly is a warm and open-hearted person. She got caught in a situation where her subtle and unconscious prejudicial thoughts bubbled to the surface. Engaging positively in diverse human interactions, to be aware and to make use of the tracker mentality to observe other humans with compassion is what is missing in our country.

Had Holly perhaps tried to learn an African language or spent some quality time with African people before her arrival at the game lodge, she would've felt far more comfortable with Thando. Even if she didn't understand his exact words, she would have most likely not reacted the way she did. It is that misunderstanding or misinterpretation of intercultural relationships that continues to plague our country.

In the early years of my relationship with Renias, I frequently experienced waves of shame and guilt – horrible emotional surges – when Renias spoke of his family's eviction, his children's almost non-existent education or his family's treatment at the hands of white people. My knee-jerk reaction was to keep telling myself that I had had nothing to do with apartheid and the ills black people faced, and I rationalised to myself that I held no responsibility for any of it.

This rationalisation did nothing for my emotional state. To try to compensate for my apparent culpability, I found myself getting unnecessarily involved in Renias's personal affairs. I tried to fix what I perceived was wrong and then tried to do what I thought would make it right. When I spoke to Renias about this many years later he simply said he knew I was trying to make myself feel better; trying to avoid the remorse associated with the past and the current collective situation.

I came to the cold realisation that my guilt was a result of how I'd benefitted materially and disproportionately from the opportunities generated by apartheid. The disparity of the situation bothered me as I had enjoyed vastly more resources growing up as a white person. I went to a good Model-C school, I had three nourishing meals a day and ultimately had access to a network of people who could protect, teach and guide me. People were inclined to afford me opportunities simply because of my appearance, my education and my ability to communicate well.

On the flip side, Renias never had the opportunity to be educated in his own language, he experienced extreme hunger and didn't have a support structure of any kind. Compared to many of my African counterparts, being born white gave me an unassailable lead in life. This made me incredibly uncomfortable and one day, while on our way to a conduct a motivational presentation, I felt compelled to formally acknowledge and apologise to Renias. As I had grown closer to the Shangaan community over the years and the more intimate I became with their collective life circumstance, the greater the shame I felt.

I told Renias I was sorry and I apologised for what my people had done. I felt I needed to do that in order to deepen my relationship with him. I didn't expect forgiveness and, indeed, Renias did not give it to me initially. Symbolically, the apology marked the end of each of our struggles with history and accepting what the past was for both of us. I knew the apology did not release me from the facts of history, but I did it because I wanted to demonstrate my commitment to an alliance, to a new order, that I sensed would be a long and productive one.

Some people have expressed their disapproval of me apologising to Renias, but it was a truthful act made in good faith and, more importantly, it marked the beginning of an honest, robust friendship that has endured many challenges in subsequent years.

Later, when I asked Renias about my apology, he said, 'I felt an ease come into my heart. And I felt much more comfortable with you.' He went on to say that the wounds of apartheid are still present in every black person and that the small acts of prejudicial behaviour by white people are noticed and they keep the wounds festering.

Being born white gives us an advantage and that comes with a certain degree of moral responsibility. People often avoid apologising to one another for fear that it will open the floodgates of reprisal, but I believe the opposite happens. Since the day of my apology to Renias, a sense of lightness and freedom entered our relationship. To say it unshackled us from the past may not be entirely accurate, but it had a radically positive impact on both our professional and personal relationship.

A good friend, Ian Schubach, invited Renias and me to Australia to take a group of bankers on a tracking safari in the Outback with two local Aboriginal trackers. During our time in the Northern Territory at King's Creek Station, we spent time tracking kangaroos, dingoes and camels, in partnership with our Aboriginal hosts, and enjoyed learning about their hunter-gatherer traditions. It wasn't long before we found out more about the many social injustices the Aboriginal people have faced in their own country, and the stark parallels to our own system of segregation. We were lucky enough to visit one of the local communities and it had a strikingly similar feel to many poor rural villages in South Africa.

When we flew out of Sydney two weeks later, comfortably seated in Premium Economy, Renias and I had an intense conversation about why so many of the 'original people' in the world have the same sad story to tell. Of course we weren't able to solve the issue, but Renias's opinion was that we need to do the best we can to stop the perpetuating cycle of poverty and despair of marginalised people. I agreed with this and do believe that our relationship is already contributing to that shift. Renias nodded his head slowly and then told me a story.

'The other day with my students we were watching a lone wildebeest bull standing in a clearing, and when I looked to the right, I saw three lionesses stalking the bull. Just then the lions charged the wildebeest, causing it to flee. As the wildebeest bolted from the fast-approaching lions, it looked back to see how close they were and in that moment the wildebeest ran into a small tree, enabling the lions to close the gap and catch up to it. The lions pounced on the poor animal and immediately killed it.'

I laughed at the way Renias re-enacted the event by pretending to run and imitate a wildebeest while looking back at the same time. I thought about it and then asked him why he was telling me that story. He said that too much 'wrong' has gone on in the world in the past, and the only way we can make a difference is to look forward. 'If South Africans keep looking back we will get killed like the wildebeest did,' he said.

Genuine transformation in South Africa will be achieved through ordinary people. To save this country we urgently need to transfer our expertise to one another. This is a complex issue, but the first step to reconciliation, I believe, is to improve the nature of our basic interactions with each other. In order to transform, we must first confront, and then let go of, egotism and fear-based ideas of 'them', and follow our inner tracks of compassion.

Renias and I will continue to focus our time working towards, and dreaming about, a future that sees people living in harmony with nature and with each other. And hopefully one day together we will be stronger together, more productive and free; living side by side with one common vision.

Appendix

The five elements of tracking

The process of finding a fresh track and following it to its conclusion and discovering the beast, is a practice that can be applied to many aspects of business and even our personal lives. It draws on a blend of what are usually considered the polar opposites of the creative and rational minds – a merging of the logical and innovative where there is little space for cognitive bias. A tracker predisposed to rational thinking, like the 'leopard man' Richard Siwela, wants to see every piece of evidence along the trail. The creative tracker looks for ways to get ahead by thinking in a completely different way. Creative thinking has the potential to give rise to a new idea while rational thought facilitates the execution of that creative idea. Tracking exercises the interplay of both. The creativity always flows from a place of deep technical competence and knowledge. Successful tracking is a steady dance between the systematic and technical with the innovative and intuitive, the emphasis being on the 'steady'. The aim is to seamlessly integrate the two processes simultaneously. To some extent our education system promotes rational thinking to the detriment of imaginative creative thought – a disparity Renias and I sometimes see in some of our tracker students.

To explain the technical process of tracking I have attempted to break it down into five of its most fundamental disciplines simply by using some of the elements that we use to evaluate practical tracking skills in the bush. As with any skill, learning to track requires you to understand its principles – the absolute essentials, such as the lead, track awareness (recognition and interpretation), track anticipation, losing the tracks and the encounter. If the basic principles are understood and practised thoroughly enough, they lose their technical hold, and over time they are internalised to the point where they become unconscious. Author of the fascinating book called *The Art of Learning*, Josh Waitzkin, who is an international chess and martial arts champion says, '[The] process of digesting small chunks of knowledge over and over again shifts it from the conscious mind to the unconscious mind where it can connect with other chunks of internalized knowledge and manifest as the sudden burst of insight we experience as free-flowing intuition.'

The lead
When discovering the first few tracks of an animal the tracker focuses on the gathering of information – the age, the number of

THE FIVE ELEMENTS OF TRACKING

other animals, gender, social make-up, speed of movement, etc. The opening piece of evidence is sometimes referred to as the lead, much the same as a lead in a crime or sales lead. The initial tracks are the oldest, usually the most weathered, and often the least obvious evidence in a string of signs left by an animal over time. Consequently, the early phases of the tracking exercise are often the most technically challenging. At the outset, the tracker aims to acquaint himself with the trail – the tracks, the substrate, the landscape and the animal's intention. This phase is slow and systematic. In the opening gambit, the tracker must carefully examine the other animals' signs that may provide confirmation of track age as well as provide greater perspective. The tracker needs to separate the fresh trail from the chaos that is the rest of the animal traffic.

During this phase, the presence of other animals' tracks may be helpful. A dove's meandering trail over a rhino's track discovered on a cold winter's morning may indicate that the rhino moved before sunset the previous evening because doves are rarely active at night, nor early on cold mornings. Or tracks of a lone buffalo bull may indicate potential danger while evidence of running zebra may suggest lions are hunting. Should the tracker overlook these seemingly unrelated bits of evidence he may stumble upon a potentially dangerous situation. All the pieces of this tracking puzzle need to be observed and remembered. But other animals' tracks can also present a challenge to a tracker if the tracks obscure the trail. Sometimes other species' signs are confusingly similar to the trail being followed, such as a hippo track on hard soil can appear remarkably similar to a rhino for a tracker not attuned to detail.

To establish a precise lead, the tracker must be hyper-focused on the detail as an early mistake can have far-reaching consequences. The tracker must possess a high-level comprehension of animal signs as well as the ability to transform the evidence into a primary insight – an initial picture of the animal's journey – in order to create a course of action.

Track awareness
Intertwined with the lead, the initial phases of the trail, is track awareness or track recognition and represents an ongoing phase of the process. It is the tracker's ability to recognise subtle and obvious physical signs and, most importantly, to interpret this evidence in the context of a specific trail on a specific substrate. The exactitude of this is key and requires a fastidious approach where something like a rhino's trail in long grass versus one left on hard soil with short grass are very different trails. A rhino trail on hard ground is characterised by intermittently evident impressions of the outside toe, sole texture or the half-moon shaped feature of the middle toenail. These are very specific pieces of physical evidence that in isolation look nothing like a rhino track but they are common signs unique to a rhino's trail in that soil type. The tracker must develop 'search images' that are unique to the trail.

While the tracker must correctly identify sign, it is as essential to discern 'the path of not here', which refers to a tracker's ability to quickly determine when a trail is no longer visible because of the animal changing direction. With lots of potentially confusing animal traffic, it is just as important for a tracker to notice where there are no tracks or if the wrong trail is being followed. The swift recognition of the absence of evidence is as equally important as recognising its presence. Being aware of the void keeps one on the trail.

Seldom does a tracker see a clear fresh track and there is no manual that depicts the specific and diverse forms of evidence related to tracking rhinos in the various soil type scenarios. Through sustained practice, the tracker teaches himself to see what is relevant and, as Renias does with the faint leopard tracks, he develops mental search images for the evidence he seeks, and then takes it a step further in recognising incomplete features of partial tracks, which makes the tracking seem almost mystical. A variety of evidence ranging from the clear and obvious to the subtle and obscure must be noticed and integrated into the trail. The tracker decides on the purpose of conducting the tracking effort, then identifies his target, gathers the data, interprets the information, and finally, puts his analysis to work by following the tracks.

Track anticipation

The third element of tracking is called track anticipation or drift. Track anticipation represents the creative and innovative form of tracking. It is a tracker's ability to maintain forward momentum in the absence of physical evidence. Track anticipation is vital to generating speed in order to close the gap. Sometimes the soil is such that it is near impossible for the tracker to perceive the tracks on the ground. Even a substantially large rhino track can disappear from sight! In this case, the tracker must predict the animal's motive by drawing on their understanding of behaviour as well as experience of tracking animals in that particular landscape. By evaluating all the signs discovered, a mental picture is formed of the activity by the track evidence, the landscape or environment and the animal itself. This is a dynamic process where success is linked to a willingness to engage with constant change, and to be open to all prospects. The three key questions a tracker is consistently asking are: What is the physical evidence saying? How is the terrain influencing the animal's movement? What is the animal doing? With time and repetition these questions become less conscious and are eventually replaced by a series of natural 'bursts of insight'. In the case of tracking a rhino on a hot day, the trail heads toward a well-worn game path and we know it recently fed and drank, taking the easiest most direct route, so we can deduce that the rhino is probably looking for a place to rest in the shaded thicket ahead. This is a simple example of the anticipation process, no different to the account of Renias discovering that leopard in a marula tree on that hot summer's day. In difficult terrain where the physical evidence is poor, the trail becomes a chain of mini predictive moments, which is in itself a skill. Accurate decision-making is something trackers must practise mastering. Animals tend to use paths of least resistance so they don't waste energy and, for this reason, learning to track barefoot is an insightful exercise for a novice tracker.

The tracker's predictive approach signifies the ability to perceive, understand and deduce, and it is essentially the execution of sound practical judgement or common sense. The rational creativity flows as a product of the reasonability, which in itself is based on deep technical competence. Local knowledge is a key ingredient to success and even expert trackers will struggle in foreign environments, like Renias and I did with the bears in America.

To anticipate successfully, the tracker's eyes must be well forward, scanning the landscape in search of its effect. Track anticipation requires the tracker to remove themselves from the detail, albeit for a while, in order to observe the big picture and the patterns in the landscape that are missed when getting unnecessarily tied up in the detail for too long. The tracks are secondary at this point. In his book *The Art of Learning*, Josh Waitzkin puts it like this: 'Numbers to leave numbers' for chess, and 'form to leave form' for Tai Chi. Similarly, track anticipation is tracking without a track – *tracks to leave tracks*. Josh explains, 'It is important to understand that by numbers to leave numbers, or form to leave form I am describing a process in which technical information is integrated into what feels like natural intelligence. Sometimes there will literally be numbers. Other times there will be principles, patterns, variations, techniques, ideas.'

At this point the tracker takes on the animal's persona, exercising their superior understanding of the animal's motivation, and perhaps even empathy for the animal. Renias always says, 'Put the animal in your heart' when referring to thinking like the animal.

Losing the tracks

The fourth element is about losing the tracks. Losing the trail happens either when the tracker loses mental or physical focus, or the substrate becomes such that the tracks are no longer visible, for example stony ground or stratum that holds the track impressions poorly, or the animal suddenly and unexpectedly changes its behaviour. Seldom will a tracker execute a trail without losing the tracks at some point; it is inevitable for all trackers, particularly those who stretch the boundaries of their capability. A lost trail is an opportunity for a tracker to deepen their understanding of animal behaviour and improve their ability to recognise obscure signs. Expert trackers do not become despondent when losing the tracks.

There are two options to deal with a lost trail. This first is to return to the last known track and painstakingly pick your way through the difficult terrain, metre by metre, until the trail becomes discernible again. This requires great attention to detail as well as patience and is the track recognition of the process. Alternatively, the tracker redefines their hypothesis (their mental picture of the animal's activity) and moves forward to test his new theory, the track anticipation aspect of the process. Dealing with a lost trail represents the review process in a campaign that has failed or is faltering. The tracker must think about what was wrong with their original positioning hypothesis and have the courage to redefine it. Making mistakes and failing are perceived as negative in Western culture, yet they are the moments of opportunity for the greatest growth. The best trackers in the world seldom make excuses; they are humble yet courageous enough to confront the facts.

The tracker must again question the situation by asking: did a change in conditions cause an altered appearance of the track impressions? Did it change direction? Did another animal walk over and obliterate the original trail? Were the tracks as fresh as originally thought? Was there an oversight like a missed interaction with another animal? The process of inquiry needs to be urgent, honest and fact-based. I've seen top trackers demonstrate a need to understand where they went wrong whereas most are content to just find the track again, without learning from their mistake. The great trackers develop a tracking culture that encourages bold self-analysis, questions and an openness to redefining their assumptions. Confronting the brutal facts is the key to successfully tracking wild animals.

I've observed trackers sweating and stressing, trying to see the next faint leopard track, desperately fixated on trying find another clear print, while a vervet monkey is alarming at the presence of the leopard no more than 100 metres away. The tracker is so single-minded that he doesn't hear the obvious and reliable signal of the monkey signposting the leopard's exact position. He's lost the trail, but he isn't giving himself the time to be soft, quiet and observant. All he needs to do is stop for a moment and he will find the leopard. He mistakenly believes that focused intensity will bring success.

The encounter
The fifth and final element is only relevant if the four other disciplines are executed properly. The encounter is the instant the tracker finds the animal he is pursuing. In an ideal situation the animal should never become aware of the tracker's presence, or at very least, not be impacted negatively by the experience. This defining moment represents an opportunity for the tracker to deepen his knowledge of the animal and its conduct. A vigilant tracker is one who is aware of the animal's needs and moves quietly with alertness and sensitivity; in many ways demonstrating compassion for the

animal he is trailing. In this scenario, the animal does not change its behaviour and the tracker is presented with a rare chance to observe it in its environment. The encounter forms an extraordinary opportunity to improve one's knowledge as the animal goes about its business without human interference. Whereas a tracker lacking in alertness has the potential to turn the encounter into a dangerous confrontation. A noisy tracker oblivious of the wind direction may easily blunder in and inadvertently cross the line of safety (minimum safe distance to an animal), causing the animal to react aggressively or flee. In this scenario, at best the animal runs away and is never seen again or at worst it charges out of the bush intent on doing grievous bodily harm. Animals react poorly to human bravado and a tracker's incompetence will almost certainly harm his would-be relationship with the animal. Experienced trackers who've spent more time than most in the presence of wild animals on foot, have had remarkably few dangerous encounters in their lives.

Successful tracking requires a combination of sound knowledge of animal behaviour and extensive, repetitive practice. Practising each of the five elements, initially in isolation and then by integrating them into a trail, will help you develop your tracking skills; which are in fact skills that can be applied to trailing animals, people and in business.

Further reading

Alcock, GG, *Third World Child: Born White, Zulu Bred*, Tracey McDonald Publishers, 2015.

Carruthers, Jane, *The Kruger National Park: A Social and Political History*, University of KwaZulu-Natal Press, 1995.

Eberhardt, Jennifer, *Biased: Uncovering the Hidden Prejudice that Shapes What We See, Think, and Do*, Penguin Random House, 2019.

Harries, P, *Slavery Amongst the Gaza Nguni: Its Changing Shape and Function and its Relationship to Other Forms of Exploitation*, 1981.

Junod, HA, *The Life of a South African Tribe*, University Publishing, 1912.

Mathebula, Mandla, *800 Years of Tsonga History: Year 1200–Year 2000*, SASAVONA Publishers and Booksellers, 2002.

Myss, Caroline, *Anatomy of the Spirit The Seven Stages of Power and Healing*, Penguin Random House, 1997.

Player, Ian, *Zululand Wilderness: Shadow and Soul*, David Philip Publishers, 1997.

Van den Heever, Alex, Mhlongo, Renias and Benadie, Karel, *A Practical Guide to Animal Tracking in Southern Africa*, Struik Nature, 2017.

Varty, Boyd, *The Lion Tracker's Guide to Life*, Houghton Mifflin, 2019.

Waitzkin, Josh, *The Art of Learning: An Inner Journey to Optimal Performance*, Free Press, 2007.

Acknowledgements

Tracking wild animals has afforded me so many opportunities that I could never have anticipated. I would like to thank Londolozi Game Reserve, all the Shangaan staff, Alan Taylor and not least the Varty family for your love and support. Shan gave me a chance when no other employer would, which I am most grateful for, and Dave has had a profound effect on the way I view the human-animal relationship.

Much gratitude to siblings Boyd and Bronwyn Varty for your committed friendship, which has seen many a season.

Thank you to the Mhlongo family who treated me as one of their own, and for the many wonderful meals, chats and laughs we have together.

I will be forever indebted to Gaynor Rupert for making Tracker Academy a reality, and to the SA College for Tourism leadership André Kilian and Mariette Ferreira for your constant guidance over the past ten years.

I am most appreciative for the hard-working and committed

trainers of Tracker Academy — Karel Benadie, Janetta Bock-Benadie, Innocent Ngwenya and Athenkosi Diba — you guys make it happen every day in the hot sun.

Thank you to Sarah Tompkins (Samara) and Gus van Dyk (Tswalu) on behalf of the Oppenheimer family who have given usage of your land for the benefit of Tracker Academy.

Many thanks to AndBeyond, Singita, Wilderness Safaris, Peace Parks Foundation, Wilderness Leadership School, Thornybush, Makuleke Contract Park, Mashatu Game Reserve, Oncafari Jaguar Project, Awasi Patagonia, African Parks Network, and Red Leaf Group for your support and for facilitating the many adventures we had together.

I am deeply appreciative to all those trackers and guides I've ever worked with for your generosity and sharing of knowledge. Thank you to Louis Liebenberg who paved the way for the recognition of trackers in this country.

Such gratitude to those friends who are more like family and have encouraged us all the way: Jerome Simonis, Rad Dougal, Heather Morrison, Raymond Mabilane, Maxine Gaines, Doc and Jenny Watson, Lawrence Weitz, Norman Chauke, Jerry Sibiye, James Tyrrell, Tom and Kate Imrie, Marnus Oshe, Elmon Sithole, Lillian Ngwenya, John and Pippa Sanderson-Smith, Debbie Marrimane, Chris Roche, Nikki Herbst, Mario Haberfeld, GG Alcock, Chris Irwin, Tony Adams, Lex Hes, James and Trish Marshall, Thobile Zulu, Meghan Walla-Murphy, Joyce Mbambo, Richard Brugman, Robert Sithole, Chris Marsicano, Phindile Rabothata, Duncan and Jess McClarty, David Dampier, Chris and Emma Goodman, Fanie Mathonse, Matt and Halszka Covarr, Linky Nkuna, Byron and Val

ACKNOWLEDGEMENTS

Ross, Seth Vorster, Graham Vercueil, Hugh and Julie Marshall, Stoff and Debbie Kane-Berman, and Sal Roux who made sure I married the right woman!

To James Hendry, the man who glared at me upon our first meeting and has become one of my closest friends and confidantes.

To the elders who have guided me so elegantly throughout my adult life: Ian and Moira Thomas, Dr Ian McCallum, Philip and Cathy van den Heever – I'm not sure what would have happened if it weren't for you!

To Andrew and Lynda Smythe for accepting me into your family with such grace.

Thank you to our favourite guests Tobe and Jack Wilson for your interest and care over the past 24 years, not to mention hundreds of great leopard sightings together.

I am grateful to Anton Lategan, a kindred spirit, for allowing me to be your partner at EcoTraining, a company that is having a significant impact on environmental consciousness in the world.

Thank you to Grant Ashfield and Ian Schubach, my partners at Wild Signs, for our inspired work in creating a tracking simulation together.

I would like to express my appreciation to Jane Bowman, who worked tirelessly and skilfully editing this book. Jane took a few campfire stories and turned them into a coherent flowing story that people will hopefully enjoy reading. I am most grateful for your time, professionalism and the grace with which you went about your work. I've bared my soul and you made it so easy.

Thank you to Reuel Khoza, GG Alcock, Sello Hatang and Max du Preez for reading the early manuscript and sharing your insights.

The list would not be complete without mentioning my old friend Renias Mhlongo who's been with me in the trenches for so long, unwavering and always positive – Ndi khensa swinene, mfo.

The story would not have happened if it weren't for all the wild animals that graciously left their trails for us to follow; it's actually all about them at the end of the day.

And finally, to my loving and unconventional parents and sister, Jon, Estelle and Missy, I love you.

Tracking Success

by Alex & Renias

In their new interactive documentary, *Tracking Success*, Alex and Renias take the ancient art of tracking to corporate conferencing where they demonstrate how the mindset of a wildlife tracker can be applied to business. Participants are divided into small teams and are then tasked with embarking on an audiovisual expedition. Immersion in the complex task of tracking and finding animals such as leopard, lion and rhino on foot is the aim and, as active participants, the team members become the trackers. Under the guidance of Alex and Renias, while at the same time working through the interactive documentary, decisions need to be made by team members. Risks need to be taken and the resultant consequences will determine whether the team successfully tracks and finds the animal.

Alex and Renias continue to conduct motivational presentations surrounding diversity and inclusiveness in the workplace. Told with humour and sensitivity, they demonstrate that the walls that isolate us from one another can be demolished. The talk is structured around three stories, which they use to extract important universal truths. The presentation demonstrates how intercultural relationships in the corporate space can lead to productive outcomes and how businesses can create a strong culture within their organisations that can have big benefits for all. The talk culminates in a few insightful and entertaining stories told by Renias in Shangaan, which Alex translates for the audience.

The duo also leads specialist tracking safaris for small groups at some of their favourite game reserves in southern Africa.

To learn more about Alex and Renias's talks, see www.alexandren.com, and for their Tracking Success virtual adventure see www.trackingsuccess.tv